SpringerBriefs in Law

More information about this series at http://www.springer.com/series/10164

Sebastián Mantilla Blanco ·
Alexander Pehl

National Security Exceptions in International Trade and Investment Agreements

Justiciability and Standards of Review

Springer

Sebastián Mantilla Blanco
Bonn, Germany

Alexander Pehl
Cologne, Germany

ISSN 2192-855X ISSN 2192-8568 (electronic)
SpringerBriefs in Law
ISBN 978-3-030-38124-0 ISBN 978-3-030-38125-7 (eBook)
https://doi.org/10.1007/978-3-030-38125-7

This Springer imprint is published by the registered company Springer Nature Switzerland AG
The registered company address is: Gewerbestrasse 11, 6330 Cham, Switzerland

Preface

National security exceptions are a usual element of international economic agreements. This holds true both for trade and investment treaties. Security clauses have been at the heart of intense academic disputes in the past. Debate has particularly revolved around the question, whether the exception has a self-judging nature and accordingly falls outside the scope of jurisdiction of international adjudicatory bodies. Whenever the conclusion is reached that a security exception is not self-judging, adjudicatory bodies will face the challenge of determining the applicable standard of review.

This work represents an effort to analyze the growing corpus of international decisions addressing this type of clauses, including WTO reports, ICJ decisions, and investment arbitral awards. It provides an overview of past and present-day tendencies in treaty drafting, identifying different generations of security exceptions.

We hope that this book will raise awareness about the variety of designs security clauses have in the field of international economic law, foster a differentiated approach to their interpretation, and contribute to a better understanding of the problems they pose in practice.

Bonn, Germany
Cologne, Germany
October 2019

Sebastián Mantilla Blanco
Alexander Pehl

Contents

Chapter 1
Introduction

Abstract Security exceptions are aimed at ensuring a margin of discretion for the adoption of sovereign decisions in questions of national security. To-date, most States consistently incorporate such exceptions into their economic treaties. Yet, treaty language has changed over time. At least three generations of security exceptions can be identified in post-Second World War trade and investment agreements. These generations broadly reflect attitudes towards trade liberalization and international decision-making, which prevailed in different historic settings.

Few words are as powerful as security. Any room for discussion ends where 'security reasons' are invoked. The call of 'security' entails a warning not to ask, not to inquire, and not to doubt. This holds true not only for police measures in airports and train stations. Security often takes on a similar role in international affairs and, more particularly, in the arena of international trade. Policy-makers too often rely on national security to justify restrictive policy choices. The past few years bear witness to the growing use of security as an ultimate means of justification. Examples appear all over the field of international economic law, from WTO disputes on the United States' imposition of tariffs on aluminum and steel[1] to investment claims on the use of India's electromagnetic spectrum.[2]

In the negotiation of international treaties, contracting States are keen to leave a door open for the adoption of measures directed at the protection of their own national security.[3] As a corollary of their use as 'escape valves',[4] the interpretation and application of security exceptions typically involve a tension between the need to

[1] Cf *United States—Steel and Aluminium Products*, DS544 (China), DS547 (India), DS548 (European Union), DS550 (Canada), DS551 (Mexico), DS552 (Norway), DS554 (Russian Federation), DS556 (Switzerland) and DS564 (Turkey).

[2] Cf. *Deutsche Telekom AG v India*, Interim Award (13 December 2017) PCA Case No. 2014-10.

[3] On the increasing use of national security exceptions in international treaties see Henckels (2019), 321 (particularly referring to investment treaties).

[4] For this terminology see Hahn (1991), 589 (particularly referring to Article XXI of the GATT).

S. Mantilla Blanco and A. Pehl, *National Security Exceptions in International Trade and Investment Agreements*, SpringerBriefs in Law,
https://doi.org/10.1007/978-3-030-38125-7_1

ensure the effectiveness of treaty obligations, on the one hand, and States' discretion and autonomy in questions of national security, on the other.[5]

Security exceptions pose two fundamental questions of treaty interpretation. First, the question arises as to whether the security exception has a self-judging character. If so, States will be the final judges of the exception's applicability. There will be no room for review of such determination by international adjudicatory bodies. Second, whenever a security clause is considered not to be self-judging, the threshold issues will be the scope of permissible review and the degree of deference owed to the sovereign State.

It is impossible to give a unique answer to these two questions. Security exceptions in economic treaties are strikingly diverse. There can thus be neither a univocal interpretation of such treaty provisions nor a single standard of review.[6] Any conclusion will depend on the language used in the applicable instrument. In its analysis of national security clauses, this study therefore departs from the manifold language employed in trade and investment agreements.

The study identifies three generations of security exceptions. These generations describe tendencies in the drafting of national security clauses, which appear as layers in the gradual development of these provisions in treaty practice. As they depict trends, different generations could overlap in some periods. Moreover, there might be security exceptions that resist classification under these categories.

The journey begins with Article XXI of the General Agreement on Tariffs and Trade (GATT) of 1947, which allows a State to adopt the measures 'it considers necessary for the protection of its essential security interests'.[7] This provision is the single most significant security clause in economic treaties concluded in the immediate aftermath of the Second World War. The wording of GATT Article XXI became a reference for subsequent treaty practice in the areas of both trade and investment. Treaty-making has since then revolved around the choice between the use of or deviation from the GATT language.

The second generation of security clauses is characterized by a pervasive optimism towards trade liberalization, the promotion of foreign investment, and international dispute settlement mechanisms. This optimism crystallized in variations of the GATT formula and a proliferation of clauses that could arguably allow a higher degree of scrutiny over security measures. This generation extended throughout a long period, albeit treaty practice was never entirely consistent. The liberal trend began with Friendship, Commerce and Navigation treaties (FCN treaties) in the 1950s, reaching its peak in the early 1990s, and gradually declining during the subsequent years.

This decline builds the bridge to the third group, which can be best depicted as the antithesis of the second generation. It is driven by the aim of ensuring the greatest possible discretion for States in matters of national security, mostly through clauses

---

[5]On the problem of balance see generally Cann (2001), 414 *et seq* (specifically addressing Article XXI of the GATT).

[6]On the need for different standards of review cf. Eisenhut (2010), 433 *et seq* and 457 *et seq*.

[7]General Agreement on Tariffs and Trade, Art. XXI(b).

which return to the GATT language. The use of this type of clauses reached a high-water mark in the 2010s. Beyond that, States are experimenting with new formulas and mechanisms. In some agreements, they have gone as far as to exclude in express terms the security exception from arbitral jurisdiction.[8] These developments reflect an emergent skepticism towards the liberal international economic system. They have a strong nexus to the uprising of nationalism, protectionism, and anti-liberal sentiments around the globe.

References

Cann WA (2001) Creating standards and accountability for the use of the WTO security exception: reducing the role of power-based relations and establishing a new balance between sovereignty and multilateralism. Yale J Int Law 26(2):413–485

Eisenhut D (2010) Sovereignty, national security and international treaty law: the standard of review of international courts and Tribunals with regard to security exceptions. AVR 48(4):431–466

Hahn M (1991) Vital interests and the law of GATT: an analysis of GATT's security exception. Mich J Int Law 12:558–620

Henckels C (2019) Investment treaty security exceptions, necessity and self-defense in context of armed conflict. In: Fach Gómez K, Gourgourinis A, Titi C (eds) international investment law and the law of armed conflict. Springer, Cham, pp 319–340

[8]Cf. particularly the examples presented in Chap. 4.

Chapter 2
The First Generation of National Security Exceptions: The GATT and Its Legacy

Abstract Article XXI of the GATT is at the heart of the first generation of security exceptions in post-Second World War economic treaties. The GATT national security exception grants a Member State discretion to adopt trade-restrictive security measures which '*it considers* necessary for the protection of its essential security interests'. An analysis of the GATT exception's wording, object and purpose, and drafting history, shows that such discretion was never intended to apply without limits.

2.1 Introductory Remarks

Article XXI of the GATT represents the core of the first generation of national security exceptions in contemporary international economic agreements. The scope and implications of this provision have been the subject of intense academic discussion for decades. The historical record suggests that, since the very inception of the GATT, there was some anxiety about possible abuses of this broadly worded security exception.[1] While this concern did not diminish with the passage of time,[2] defenses based on Article XXI of the GATT were a true rarity for decades.[3] Therefore, at least to some extent, the security exception was largely perceived as a sleeping dog.[4]

The past few years might be the turning point. The Trump Administration invoked national security as justification for trade-restrictive measures in different sectors.[5] The Russian Federation also relied on national security as a means to defend some

[1] See UN Economic and Social Council, Second Session of the Preparatory Committee of the United Nations Conference on Trade and Employment, Verbatim Report, Thirty-Third Meeting of Commission A, 24 July 1947, E/PC/T/A/PV/33, 21; WTO, Analytical Index of the GATT (pre-1995), 600. Cf. also Deutscher Bundestag (2018), 6.

[2] Bhala (1998), 268 *et seq*; Alexandroff and Sharma (2005), 1572.

[3] Alexandroff and Sharma (2005), 1572.

[4] Cf. however the GATT cases involving defenses under GATT Art. XXI in Sect. 2.3.1.

[5] On these measures as elements of the Trump Administration's trade policy cf. Koh (2019), 57 *et seq*; cf. also Sects. 2.3.2 and 2.6.

S. Mantilla Blanco and A. Pehl, *National Security Exceptions in International Trade and Investment Agreements*, SpringerBriefs in Law,
https://doi.org/10.1007/978-3-030-38125-7_2

of the most controversial economic measures adopted against Ukraine.[6] As requests for consultations were brought before the WTO, this highly political issue gave rise to legal disputes about the interpretation and application of Article XXI of the GATT.[7] In April 2019, the WTO Panel in *Russia—Traffic in Transit* delivered the first detailed assessment of a defense under Article XXI in the history of the WTO.[8] Other cases are still pending.[9] The following sections explore the origins, structure, and interpretation of the GATT security exception. In this vein, they draw particular attention to the analysis delivered in the Panel Report of April 2019.[10]

2.2 Article XXI of the GATT: A Brief Overview

International trade law pursues the liberalization of trade and the elimination of protectionism through the reduction of barriers to the international exchange of goods and services.[11] Most trade agreements seek to strike a balance between this general goal of liberalization, on the one hand, and national interests which might be inconsistent with such purpose on the other.[12] Exceptions to treaty obligations are the main tools for achieving such balance, as they provide what has been described as '[a] breathing space for the exercise of State sovereignty'.[13] In the framework of the GATT, Article XX establishes a set of general exceptions which allows WTO Members to adopt measures that would be otherwise contrary to substantive obligations under the treaty.[14] Article XX requires that these measures pursue the protection of specific interests (such as public morals or human health), and fulfill the general conditions set forth in the provision's *chapeau*.[15] Besides the general exceptions, Article XXI of the GATT authorizes the adoption of measures directed at the protection of a Member's national security:

> Nothing in this Agreement shall be construed
>
> (a) to require any contracting party to furnish any information the disclosure of which it considers contrary to its essential security interests; or

---

[6]Cf. *Russia—Measures Concerning Traffic in Transit*, Report of the Panel (5 April 2019) WT/DS512/R.

[7]Cf. Sect. 2.3.2.

[8]Cf. *Russia—Measures Concerning Traffic in Transit*, Report of the Panel (5 April 2019) WT/DS512/R, paras 7.72 *et seq.* A scholar writing on the subject states that, with the Russian case, 'Pandora's box has been opened', Bogdanova (2019).

[9]For a description of these cases see Sect. 2.3.2.

[10]*Russia—Measures Concerning Traffic in Transit*, Report of the Panel (5 April 2019) WT/DS512/R.

[11]See Herdegen (2016), Chap. XIV.1. On the goals of the WTO cf. Jackson (2006), 84 *et seq.*

[12]See generally Hahn (1991), 561 *et seq.*

[13]Hahn (1991), 562.

[14]Cf. Koul (2018), 341 *et seq.*

[15]See generally *ibid.*

(b) to prevent any contracting party from taking any action which it considers necessary for the protection of its essential security interests

(i) relating to fissionable materials or the materials from which they are derived;

(ii) relating to the traffic in arms, ammunition and implements of war and to such traffic in other goods and materials as is carried on directly or indirectly for the purpose of supplying a military establishment;

(iii) taken in time of war or other emergency in international relations; or

(c) to prevent any contracting party from taking any action in pursuance of its obligations under the United Nations Charter for the maintenance of international peace and security.[16]

While this study will focus on Article XXI(b), some brief remarks about *lit.* a and c might help visualize the overall assembly of the GATT security exception.[17] Article XXI(a) protects Member States' prerogative to refuse disclosure of information that could affect their essential security interests. A representative of the US Department of War, Howard H. Neff, suggested this exception during the negotiations of the Charter of the International Trade Organization (ITO Charter) in 1947.[18] Neff's purpose was to prevent the US Government from entering into an obligation to disclose classified or otherwise sensible data.[19] This would be the case, for example, where information could potentially reveal the identity of sources of intelligence.[20] It has been argued that Article XXI(a), albeit granting the State a certain margin of discretion, requires the existence of 'objective circumstances' indicating a threat to essential security interests.[21] In this sense, it is argued, the State enjoys broad discretion but must still be able to provide a reasonable justification for a refusal of disclosure.[22]

Article XXI(c) expresses the fundamental idea that obligations under Chapter VII of the UN Charter prevail over obligations under the GATT.[23] This principle is in line with Article 103 of the UN Charter and, hence, fosters coherence in the institutional and legal arrangements of the postwar international community.[24] Academic studies have concluded that Article XXI(c) poses no issues of justiciability because the existence of the obligation triggering the exception is a legal question, which adjudicators can and should ascertain in objective terms.[25]

---

[16]General Agreement on Tariffs and Trade, Art. XXI. For a general overview of GATT Article XXI see Matsushita et al. (2015), 548 *et seq.*

[17]On the structure of the security exception see generally Hahn (1996), 285 *et seq.*

[18]See Vandevelde (2017), 147.

[19]See *ibid.*

[20]Cf. Bhala (1998), 276.

[21]See Hahn (1996), 292.

[22]*Ibid.*

[23]See generally Herrmann et al. (2007), 349 *et seq.*

[24]Charter of the United Nations (adopted 26 June 1945, entered into force 24 October 1945) Art. 103.

[25]van den Bossche (2008), 669.

The heart of the GATT security exception is Article XXI(b).[26] The provision covers three different situations.[27] These scenarios are 'fissionable materials', 'traffic in arms', and 'war or other emergency in international relations'.[28] For present purposes, particular attention must be drawn to the third scenario. The term 'war' points to the concept of 'armed conflict'.[29] The notion of 'armed conflict' in international law has significantly evolved over the past decades, covering classic inter-State conflicts as well as non-international conflicts, and further adapting to new forms of warfare (e.g. cyber-warfare).[30]

The interpretation of the GATT security exception must depart from the fundamental premise that not every international tension or conflict, however severe, fits into the categories of 'war' or 'other emergency in international relations'.[31] The phrase 'or other' implies that 'war' is a subcategory of the broader notion of 'emergency in international relations'.[32] Yet, the phrase 'emergency in international relations' is strikingly vague and could give rise to divergent interpretations.[33] The fact that this phrase appears in context with the notion of 'war' suggests that it refers only to truly exceptional situations.[34] As the Panel in *Russia—Traffic in Transit* pointed out, an 'emergency in international relations' must be understood 'as eliciting the same type of interests as those arising from the other matters addressed in the enumerated subparagraphs of Article XXI(b)'.[35]

While the three scenarios covered by Article XXI(b) refer to different situations, they have some common threads. Importantly, the measures justified under the exception shall be 'consider[ed] necessary for the protection of [...] essential security interests'.[36] The meaning of this sentence remains a most contentious issue.[37] There seems to be some agreement on the idea that the provision covers at least those interests that affect the political and military affairs of the contracting parties.[38] Some

---

[26]See Bhala (1998), 267.

[27]See Hahn (1996), 294.

[28]General Agreement on Tariffs and Trade, Art. XXI(b)(i)-(iii).

[29]*Russia—Measures Concerning Traffic in Transit*, Report of the Panel (5 April 2019) WT/DS512/R, para 7.72.

[30]Herdegen (2019), § 34 para 23 and § 56 paras 4 *et seq*. Cf. also Glöckle (2019), 659; Slawotsky (2018), 233. For a detailed analysis of cyber-warfare in international law see Schulze (2015), 7 *et seq*.

[31]On these two categories cf. Hahn (1996), 345 *et seq*.

[32]*Russia—Measures Concerning Traffic in Transit*, Report of the Panel (5 April 2019) WT/DS512/R, para 7.72.

[33]See Hahn (1996), 350 *et seq*.

[34]*Ibid*., 349.

[35]*Russia—Measures Concerning Traffic in Transit*, Report of the Panel (5 April 2019) WT/DS512/R, para 7.74.

[36]General Agreement on Tariffs and Trade, Art. XXI(b).

[37]Cf. Sects. 2.4 and 2.5.

[38]Hahn (1996), 295.

authors have suggested that, read in context, Article XXI(b) primarily refers to the external security of the State.[39]

In any case, the interests protected through security measures must be 'essential'. This implies that the exception does not cover every national security interest.[40] As a rule, this requirement will be fulfilled at least where a situation of fact involves a 'threat or use of force against the territorial integrity or political independence of any State' in violation of Article 2(4) of the UN Charter.[41]

The concept of 'essential security interests' is certainly wide, but not without limits. It is a common place that this wording excludes interests which have a mere economic or commercial character.[42] The enumeration provided in Article XXI(b)(i) to (iii) of the GATT is closely related to the notions of armed conflict and physical security.[43] However, it is not always possible to draw a sharp line between pure economic interests and non-economic interests. The gradual expansion of the notion of security over the past decades might pose a challenge for the interpretation and application of the security exception.[44] National security is not considered to exclusively refer to physical or military threats to a State's integrity, but is generally conceived as a broad notion that encompasses non-military threats too.[45] Thus, economic emergencies are often characterized as national security issues.[46]

In addition, there are industry sectors which involve or affect national security in the most traditional sense of the term.[47] For example, defense capabilities may be to some extent dependent on a proper functioning of the steel industry.[48] The allied occupation of the *Ruhrgebiet*—the historic center of German steel and heavy

---

[39] *Ibid.*, 295 *et seq.*

[40] Cf. *ibid.*, 297. The essentiality requirement has also been discussed in the context of investment arbitral proceedings, cf. *Deutsche Telekom AG v India*, Interim Award (13 December 2017) PCA Case No. 2014-10, para 236.

[41] Charter of the United Nations (adopted 26 June 1945, entered into force 24 October 1945) Art. 2(4). For this interpretation of Art. XXI(b) of the GATT see Hahn (1996), 297.

[42] See already the statement of the delegate of the United States, JM Leddy, UN Economic and Social Council, Second Session of the Preparatory Committee of the United Nations Conference on Trade and Employment, Verbatim Report, Thirty-Third Meeting of Commission A (24 July 1947) E/PC/T/A/PV/33, 20 *et seq.* Cf. also Hahn (1996), 295 *et seq.*

[43] Cf. *Russia—Measures Concerning Traffic in Transit*, Report of the Panel (5 April 2019) WT/DS512/R, para 7.75.

[44] See Desierto (2012), 146.

[45] *Ibid.* Cf. also Lee (2018), 301–2 (arguing that GATT Article XXI could cover some 'commercial situations').

[46] Desierto (2012), 146.

[47] Cf. Hahn (1991), 560–1 and 581 (referring to the case of 'key industries').

[48] Sweden sought to justify measures directed at the protection of the local footwear industry in 1975 on grounds of national security and, in 2018, the United States used the exception to justify measures protecting the national production of steel and aluminum. See *Sweden—Import Restrictions on Certain Footwear*, Notification by the Swedish Delegation (17 November 1975) L/4250 and *United States—Certain Measures on Steel and Aluminium Products*, WT/DS544, DS547, DS548, DS550, DS551, DS552, DS554, DS556 and DS564.

industry—in the aftermath of the First World War bears witness to the strong link between these industries and national security.[49]

Even with regard to such industries, the application of Article XXI(b) remains exceptional. This exceptional character becomes clear in the interplay between the security exception and other GATT provisions. Thus, Article XIX of the GATT (escape clause) allows the contracting parties—under certain strict conditions—to adopt 'emergency measures' where imports pose a threat of 'serious injury' to their national industries.[50] GATT Article XXI(b) should not become a means to circumvent more specific rules about the protection of national industries of significant importance, such as Article XIX.[51]

2.3 The GATT Security Exception in Practice

2.3.1 Setting the Scene: The GATT Years

Prior to the establishment of the WTO in 1994, at least nine disputes involved defenses based on Article XXI of the GATT.[52] As will be shown throughout this section, GATT practice did never deliver a detailed assessment of the content and scope of the security exception. There were, however, some instances in which the exception was portrayed in terms which came close to its characterization as a self-judging provision.[53] Thus, in June 1949, during a meeting held in a hotel in the French city of Annecy, representatives of different GATT contracting parties discussed a complaint submitted by Czechoslovakia against the United States.[54] In an often-quoted statement, the representative of the British Government, Mr. Shacke, observed:

> [E]very country must have the last resort on questions related to its own security. On the other hand, CONTRACTING PARTIES should be cautious not to take any step which might have the effect of undermining the General Agreement.[55]

---

[49]On the occupation see generally: Krummeich and Schröder (2004); Emmes (2019), 146 *et seq.*

[50]General Agreement on Tariffs and Trade, Art. XIX. On the interpretation of this provision cf. WTO, WTO Analytical Index, Art. XIX.

[51]Hahn (1996), 300 *et seq.*

[52]For an overview see Alexandroff and Sharma (2005), 1574 *et seq*; Pelc (2016), 101 *et seq*; Hahn (1996), 319–342; Mavroidis (2005), 214–223. For a detailed presentation of these cases (discussed below) see WTO, Analytical Index of the GATT (pre-1995), Art. XXI (at 600 *et seq*).

[53]Cf. generally the discussion of pre-WTO State practice in Alford (2011), 706 *et seq* (focusing on GATT practice).

[54]GATT Contracting Parties, Third Session, Summary Record of the 22nd Meeting (8 June 1949) CP.3/SR22—II/28, wto.org/english/tratop_e/dispu_e/gatt_e/49expres.pdf, accessed 1 September 2019.

[55]*Ibid.*, 3. Cf. also GATT, CP.3/SR.22, Corr 1, both quoted in WTO, Analytical Index of the GATT (pre-1995), 600.

A similar understanding of the exception appears in the documents pertaining to the suspension of the import of Argentinean products into Australia, Canada and the European Economic Communities (ECC) during the Falkland/Malvinas conflict, in 1982.[56] As the measure was justified on Article XXI of the GATT, the focus of the Council deliberations was precisely the scope of permissible review under the national security exception.[57] The record suggests that representatives of several parties considered that the clause was self-judging. The representative of the European Communities argued that the exercise of the rights set forth in Article XXI of the GATT was a prerogative subject to the sole judgment of each Contracting Party.[58] Similarly, the Canadian Government expressed the view that the GATT was not the appropriate forum for this question, which it depicted as a 'political issue'.[59] More explicitly, the representative of the US Government stated:

> [T]he GATT had no role in a crisis of military force. The General Agreement left to each contracting party the judgment as to what it considered to be necessary to protect its security interests. The Contracting Parties had no power to question that judgment.[60]

A new dispute on the self-judging character of GATT Article XXI arose a few years later, in the *United States—Trade Measures affecting Nicaragua* dispute of 1985.[61] The case concerned the Reagan Administration's decision to prohibit imports from as well as exports to Nicaragua.[62] The Nicaraguan Government filed a request for the establishment of a Panel.[63] Nicaragua departed from the premise that the existence of a situation of emergency under Article XXI of the GATT, such as a war, was a justiciable issue.[64] A Panel was actually established, but its scope of jurisdiction was defined to the exclusion of '[the] validity or motivation for the invocation of Article XXI(b)(iii) by the United States'.[65] The Panel Report, which was never adopted, was clear in stating that it made no assessment of or finding about this specific question.[66]

Against this backdrop, GATT practice sheds little light on the standard of review, if any, applicable under the security exception. Still, the debates from those years are useful examples of the type of situations in which the exception could be invoked.

---

[56]Communication to the Members of the GATT Council (1982).

[57]WTO, Analytical Index of the GATT (pre-1995), 600 (citing the statements of the ECC, Canada, Australia, the US, and Argentina).

[58]Cf. *ibid.*

[59]GATT Council, Minutes of the Meeting of 07 May 1982, C/M/157, 10.

[60]GATT Council, Minutes of the Meeting of 29–30 June 1982, C/M/159, 19.

[61]*United States—Trade Measures affecting Nicaragua*, Report of the Panel (13 October 1986) L/6053 (not adopted).

[62]*Ibid.*, paras 3.1 *et seq.*

[63]Cf. *ibid.*, para 4.1.

[64]*United States—Trade Measures affecting Nicaragua*, Communication from Nicaragua (8 May 1985) L/5802; GATT Council, Minutes of the Meeting of 17–19 July 1985, C/M/191, 43; see also WTO, Analytical Index of the GATT (pre-1995), 603.

[65]GATT Council, Minutes of the Meeting of 12 March 1986, C/M/196, 7.

[66]*United States—Trade Measures affecting Nicaragua*, Report of the Panel (13 October 1986) L/6053 (not adopted), para 5.3.

In very rare instances, the exception was used to justify the protection of national industries in situations involving no specific political or military crisis. For example, Sweden relied on the security exception enshrined in Article XXI of the GATT to justify an import quota on footwear in 1975.[67] Swedish representatives argued that a domestic footwear industry was necessary to satisfy the demand of the armed forces and, by implication, to protect the State's essential security interests.[68] The Swedish Government would finally revoke this controversial measure.[69]

By contrast to the Swedish case, most relevant GATT disputes did actually refer to economic measures adopted in the context of complex political tensions. Some of these tensions were on the spot of world politics. The Falkland/Malvinas conflict of 1982 and the US-Nicaragua dispute of 1985 can serve as representative examples to this effect.[70] In light of the political and military interests at stake, States were too-often unwilling to submit the interpretation of the security exception to the decision of a GATT Panel. The narrow scope of the jurisdiction given to the Panel in the Nicaragua case of 1985 provides a clear example of this reluctance.[71]

In the GATT years, there were several instances in which measures were initially justified under the security exception, but there was never an actual discussion about the meaning and scope of Article XXI. In some cases, the bold question was whether the GATT could be truly regarded as an appropriate forum for issues of national security. These doubts appeared, for example, in the context of the sanctions imposed by the EEC on Yugoslavia in the early 1990s.[72] In its meeting of 10 April 1992, the GATT Council discussed Yugoslavia's request to constitute a Panel.[73] Members agreed that Yugoslavia had a right to file the request, but opinions were divided as to the suitability of such proceedings for the settlement of the dispute.[74]

2.3.2 The Renaissance of the Security Exception in WTO Practice

The establishment of the WTO in 1995 coincided with a climate of widespread optimism towards the liberalization of international trade: The fall of the Berlin Wall was still a fresh memory and there was unshakeable faith in the self-regulating

[67] Cf. *Sweden—Import Restrictions on Certain Footwear*, Notification by the Swedish Delegation (17 November 1975) L/4250.

[68] *Ibid.*

[69] Alexandroff and Sharma (2005), 1574.

[70] Cf. Communication to the Members of the GATT Council (1982).

[71] Cf. GATT Council, Minutes of the Meeting of 12 March 1986, C/M/196, 7.

[72] Cf. GATT, Minutes of the Meeting held in the Centre William Rappard on 18 March 1992, C/M/255 (10 April 1992).

[73] *Ibid.*, 14–18.

[74] *Ibid.* Cf. also Mavroidis (2012), 374.

power of markets.[75] In 1989, Francis Fukuyama famously coined the term 'end of history', arguing that humanity had conclusively reached the final stage of historical development with an 'unabashed victory of economic and political liberalism'.[76]

In this liberal stage, it seems little surprising that States rarely invoked the security exception. Before the 2010s, the perhaps most relevant case was a complaint of the EEC regarding the extension of the US embargo on Cuba through the Cuban Liberty and Democratic Solidarity Act of 1996, best known as the Helms-Burton Act.[77] The United States relied on Article XXI of the GATT, further announcing its decision not to attend the Panel proceedings.[78] The Panel was still established, but no report was issued in the end.[79] Deliberations and reciprocal concessions led the European Communities to finally request suspension of the proceedings.[80] Acknowledging some sense of restraint of States regarding the exception, academic studies proclaimed that the fears about potential abuses of GATT Article XXI were largely unfounded.[81]

The situation changed in 2016, as a Panel was constituted in a case involving a defense based on GATT Article XXI.[82] In *Russia—Traffic in Transit*, the Government of Ukraine alleged a violation of WTO law resulting from certain restrictions on traffic in transit implemented by the Russian Federation.[83] Russia conceived the restriction, which affected exports from the Ukraine into countries in Central Asia, as a response to the so-called 'Euromaidan' (i.e. the gradual legal, economic, and political approximation of Ukraine to the European Union).[84]

In its response to the Ukrainian request for consultations, the Russian Government presented a defense which essentially focused on the national security exception of Article XXI(b)(iii) of the GATT.[85] Russia specifically argued that the measures in

---

[75] For a critical discussion of the expectations about the role of the WTO cf. Goldsmith and Posner (2005) 158 *et seq.*

[76] Fukuyama (1989). Cf. also Fukuyama (1992), xi *et seq.* In a recent publication, Fukuyama reflects on his own approach in light of the present-day political reality: Fukuyama (2018) xii *et seq.*

[77] *United States—The Cuban Liberty and Democratic Solidarity Act*, Request for the Establishment of a Panel by the European Communities (8 October 1996) WT/DS38/2.

[78] Sanger (1997); Alexandroff and Sharma (2005), 1576.

[79] *United States—The Cuban Liberty and Democratic Solidarity Act*, Constitution of the Panel Established at the Request of the European Communities (20 February 1997) WT/DS38/3. On the debate cf. Spagnole (1998), 1313 *et seq.*

[80] *United States—The Cuban Liberty and Democratic Solidarity Act*, Communication from the Chairman of the Panel (25 April 1997) WT/DS38/5.

[81] Alford (2011), 758. See also Lindsay (2003), 1312.

[82] *Russia—Measures Concerning Traffic in Transit of Ukrainian Products*, Request for Consultations by Ukraine (21 September 2016) WT/DS512/1, G/L/1151; *Russia—Measures Concerning Traffic in Transit of Ukrainian Products*, Constitution of the Panel Established at the Request of Ukraine (7 June 2017) WT/DS512/4. On this rupture with the restrictive use of the security exception see Glöckle (2019), 653–654.

[83] *Russia—Measures Concerning Traffic in Transit*, Report of the Panel (5 April 2019) WT/DS512/R, paras 7.1 *et seq.*

[84] *Ibid.*, paras 7.5 *et seq.*

[85] *Ibid.*, paras 7.3 *et seq.*

question were aimed at countering a threat to its essential security interests.[86] Based on this contention, Russia claimed that the Panel lacked jurisdiction to evaluate the security measures challenged by Ukraine.[87] For its part, Ukraine submitted that Article XXI(b)(iii) of the GATT was not intended to grant the invoking Member State 'total discretion' and that the Panel was therefore competent to conduct an objective assessment of the security clause's requirements, including the requisite that the security measures be adopted in good faith.[88] Seventeen Members of the WTO joined the proceedings as third parties.[89] In its Third-Party Submission, the US expressed support for the Russian characterization of the security clause as a self-judging exception.[90] The other third parties took the opposite view, siding with Ukraine's line of argument.[91]

In April 2019, the Panel in *Russia—Traffic in Transit* declared that its jurisdiction extended over the security exception.[92] In the exercise of this jurisdiction, the Panel found that GATT Article XXI(b)(iii) covered the measures adopted by the Russian Federation.[93] This decision was of major importance not only because of its outcome but, perhaps more importantly, because it established that the application of the national security exception was subject to the scrutiny of WTO adjudicating bodies.[94]

The case of *Russia—Traffic in Transit* was just the beginning of a series of recent cases involving Article XXI of the GATT.[95] The US tariffs on aluminum and steel

---

[86] *Ibid.*, para 7.4.

[87] *Ibid.*, para 3.2.

[88] *Ibid.*, para 7.33.

[89] That is: Australia, Bolivia, Brazil, Canada, Chile, China, the European Union, India, Japan, Korea, Moldova, Norway, Paraguay, Saudi Arabia, Singapore, Turkey, and the United States (*ibid.*, para 1.6).

[90] *Russia—Measures Concerning Traffic in Transit of Ukrainian Products*, WT/DS512, Third Party Executive Summary of the United States of America (27 February 2018); cf. *Russia—Measures Concerning Traffic in Transit*, Report of the Panel (5 April 2019) WT/DS512/R, paras 7.51 *et seq.*

[91] *Russia—Measures Concerning Traffic in Transit*, Report of the Panel (5 April 2019) WT/DS512/R, paras 7.35 *et seq*; see also the submissions of Australia and the European Union: *Russia—Measures Concerning Traffic in Transit of Ukrainian Products*, WT/DS512, Third Party Written Submission of the European Union (8 November 2017); *Russia—Measures Concerning Traffic in Transit of Ukrainian Products*, WT/DS512, Third Party Oral Statement by the European Union (25 January 2018); *Russia—Measures Concerning Traffic in Transit of Ukrainian Products*, WT/DS512, Third Party Oral Statement of Australia (25 January 2018).

[92] *Russia—Measures Concerning Traffic in Transit*, Report of the Panel (5 April 2019) WT/DS512/R, para 8.1(a)(i).

[93] *Ibid.*, para 8.2.

[94] *Ibid.*, paras 7.53 *et seq*. On the significance of the Panel report see also Glöckle (2019), 652, 655 and 658–659.

[95] For example: *Ukraine—Measures Relating to Trade in Goods and Services*, WT/DS525; *United Arab Emirates—Measures Relating to Trade in Goods and Services, and Trade Related Aspects of IP Rights*, WT/DS526; *United States—Certain Measures on Steel and Aluminium Products*, WT/DS544, DS547, DS548, DS550, DS551, DS552, DS554, DS556 and DS564; *Russia—Measures on the Importation of Live Pigs, Pork and Other Pig Products from the European Union*, WT/DS475.

resulted in the filing of nine WTO complaints.[96] A large number of third parties have joined the proceedings, turning the dispute into a true question of general interest.[97] The complaining Members have argued that the US measures were in breach of several provisions of the GATT and of the Agreement on Safeguards.[98] The US Government submitted almost identically worded communications in the proceedings, consistently claiming that the tariffs constituted a measure necessary for the protection of its essential security interests.[99] In its response to the request for consultations filed by the Chinese Government, the US drew the following argument:

> China's request concerns tariffs on imports of steel and aluminum articles imposed by the President of the United States pursuant to Section 232 of the Trade Expansion Act of 1962 [...]. The President determined that tariffs were necessary to adjust the imports of steel and aluminum articles that threaten to impair the national security of the United States. Issues of national security are political matters not susceptible to review or capable of resolution by WTO dispute settlement. Every Member of the WTO retains the authority to determine for itself those matters that it considers necessary to the protection of its essential security interests, as is reflected in the text of Article XXI of the GATT 1994.[100]

The central issue in these cases is whether WTO dispute settlement bodies may review a Member State's reliance on Article XXI of the GATT and, if so, whether the United States have complied with the requirements of the national security exception.[101] It remains to be seen whether future Panels and perhaps the WTO Appellate Body will confirm the conclusions reached in *Russia—Traffic in Transit*. The contention that the US measures serve mere commercial purposes, as some commentators suggest, promises to sow further controversy.[102]

---

[96] *United States—Steel and Aluminium Products*, DS544 (China), DS547 (India), DS548 (European Union), DS550 (Canada), DS551 (Mexico), DS552 (Norway), DS554 (Russian Federation), DS556 (Switzerland) and DS564 (Turkey).

[97] For instance, China was joined by Bahrain, Brazil, Canada, Colombia, Egypt, the European Union, Guatemala, Hong Kong, Iceland, India, Indonesia, Japan, Kazakhstan, Malaysia, Mexico, New Zealand, Norway, Qatar, Russian Federation, Saudi Arabia, Singapore, South Africa, Switzerland, Chinese Taipei, Thailand, Turkey, Ukraine, and Venezuela. See *United States—Certain Measures on Steel and Aluminium Products*, WT/DS544, case overview, wto.org/english/tratop_e/dispu_e/cases_e/ds544_e.htm, accessed 1 September 2019.

[98] See *United States—Certain Measures on Steel and Aluminium Products*, Request for the Establishment of a Panel by China (19 October 2018) WT/DS544/8.

[99] Cf., for example, *United States—Certain Measures on Steel and Aluminium Products*, Communication from the United States (13 April 2018) WT/DS544/2.

[100] *Ibid.*

[101] For an overview of ongoing disputes involving the GATT security exception see Voon (2019), 46 *et seq.*

[102] Charnovitz (2018), Lester (2018), Weiler (2018).

2.4 Review of Security Measures Under Article XXI of the GATT and the Problem of Justiciability

As with most security exceptions, the interpretation of GATT Article XXI(b) must address at least two major questions.[103] The first question, which is also the one that has attracted most scholarly attention, is whether, as some States and commentators have claimed,[104] Article XXI(b) is self-judging. This question devolves into a debate on the possibility of using the security exception as a jurisdictional defense.[105] The second question only arises where the first question is given a negative answer, and pertains to the scope of review permissible under the exception.[106]

The justiciability of the GATT security exception is one of the most divisive issues of contemporary trade law. State practice is not uniform and cannot be said to indicate an agreement among WTO Members on the interpretation of Article XXI(b) of the GATT, in the sense of Article 31(3)(b) of the Vienna Convention on the Law of Treaties (VCLT).[107] There is moreover great diversity of opinions about the often-claimed self-judging character of the security clause.[108]

Scholars have argued that Article XXI GATT is an exception to material standards and not to dispute settlement provisions.[109] Just as the general exceptions of GATT Article XX,[110] Article XXI provides a normative basis to justify measures that are inconsistent with other treaty provisions.[111] As explained by the Panel in *United States—Section 337 of the Tariff Act of 1930*, these exceptions come into play only when it has been established that a measure is incompatible with an obligation under the GATT:

---

[103]Cf. also the analysis of these two questions with regard to investment treaties in Sects. 3.2.2 and 3.2.3.

[104]For some indicative examples see Alford (2011), 697 *et seq*; Bhala (1998), 268 *et seq*; Burke-White and von Staden (2008), 376 *et seq*. Cf. also *Russia—Measures Concerning Traffic in Transit of Ukrainian Products*, WT/DS512, Third Party Executive Summary of the United States of America (27 February 2018); *CC/Devas (Mauritius) Ltd., Devas Employees Mauritius Private Limited, Telecom Devas Mauritius Limited*, Award (25 July 2016) PCA Case No. 2013-09, para 219 n 286.

[105]See generally: Schloemann and Ohlhoff (1999), 431 *et seq*. Cf. also the discussion in Anuradha (2018), 313 *et seq*.

[106]See Sect. 2.5.

[107]*Russia—Measures Concerning Traffic in Transit*, Report of the Panel (5 April 2019) WT/DS512/R, para 7.80. In *Russia—Measures Concerning Traffic in Transit*, the Panel reached this conclusion based on an in-depth analysis of subsequent practice, which was attached as an Appendix to the Report. Cf. *Russia—Measures Concerning Traffic in Transit*, Report of the Panel (5 April 2019) WT/DS512/R, 106 *et seq* ('Appendix—Subsequent Conduct Concerning Article XXI of the GATT 1947').

[108]Balan (2018), 2.

[109]Balan (2018), 5.

[110]On the drafting history of GATT Articles XX and XXI see WTO, Analytical Index of the GATT (pre-1995), 608.

[111]For an overview cf. Mavroidis (2012), 84.

> The Panel noted that Article XX is entitled 'General Exceptions' and that the central phrase in the introductory clause reads: "nothing in this Agreement shall be construed to prevent the adoption or enforcement … of measures …". Article XX(d) thus provides for a limited and conditional exception from obligations under other provisions. The Panel therefore concluded that Article XX(d) applies only to measures inconsistent with another provision of the General Agreement, and that, consequently, the application of Section 337 has to be examined first in the light of Article III:4. If any inconsistencies with Article III:4 were found, the Panel would then examine whether they could be justified under Article XX(d).[112]

This idea cannot be reconciled with an understanding of Article XXI of the GATT as a jurisdictional defense. If Article XXI were to exclude jurisdiction, there would be no opportunity to determine the inconsistency of a measure with a substantive provision of the GATT in the first place.[113] Nothing in the WTO Agreement indicates that the security exception is excluded from the scope of application of the dispute settlement provisions of the GATT and the Dispute Settlement Understanding (DSU).[114] During the drafting process of the GATT, a US delegate was explicit in stating that the dispute settlement clauses of the General Agreement were applicable with regard to the national security clause:

> [If an action] even though not in conflict with the terms of Article 94 [now Article XXI GATT], should affect another Member, I should think that that Member would have the right to seek redress of some kind under Article 35 [now Articles XXII and XXIII GATT] as it now stands. In other words, there is no exception from the application of Article 35 to this or any other Article.[115]

The text of Articles XXII and XXIII of the GATT indicates, in fact, that no GATT provision is excluded from dispute settlement.[116] Article XXII(1) of the GATT vests the Member States with the possibility of seeking consultations 'with respect to *any matter* affecting the operation of this Agreement'.[117] Article XXIII GATT provides for a special procedure for reaching an adjustment between WTO Members where 'any contracting party should consider that any benefit accruing to it directly or indirectly under this Agreement is being nullified or impaired or that the attainment of any objective of the Agreement is being impeded'.[118]

This is consistent with the *Decision Concerning Article XXI of the General Agreement* of 1982, which establishes with paramount clarity that 'when action is taken under Article XXI, all contracting parties affected by such action retain their full

---

[112] *United States—Section 337 of the Tariff Act of 1930*, Report of the Panel (7 November 1989) L/6439-36S/345, para 5.9.

[113] On the structure of exceptions and the determination of the burden of proof see Benzing (2010), 644 *et seq* (particularly analyzing the WTO Agreement).

[114] See *Russia—Measures Concerning Traffic in Transit of Ukrainian Products*, WT/DS512, Third Party Written Submission of the European Union (8 November 2017) 4.

[115] Second Session of the Preparatory Committee of the United Nations Conference on Trade and Employment, Verbatim Report, Thirty-Third Meeting (24 July 1947) E/PC/T/A/PV/33, 26 *et seq.*

[116] Cf. GATT Arts. XXII and XXIII.

[117] GATT Art. XXII(1) (emphasis added).

[118] Cf. GATT Art. XXIII.

rights under the General Agreement'.[119] The fact that measures invoking Article XXI of the GATT were the subject of dispute settlement procedures prior to the establishment of the WTO (e.g. the Czechoslovak complaint filed under Article XXIII of the GATT against US export controls in 1949),[120] suggests this premise enjoyed fairly broad acceptance.[121]

In its third-party submission in the case *Russia—Traffic in Transit*, the European Union rightly pointed out that 'interpreting Article XXI of GATT 1994 as a non-justiciable provision in this dispute would be inconsistent with the terms of reference of the Panel'.[122] In this vein, the EU specifically referred to Article 7(1) and 7(2) of the DSU[123]:

> 7. Terms of reference of Panels.
>
> 1. Panels shall have the following terms of reference unless the parties to the dispute agree otherwise within 20 days from the establishment of the panel:
>
>   "To examine, in the light of the relevant provisions in (name of the covered agreement(s) cited by the parties to the dispute), the matter referred to the DSB by (name of party) in document … and to make such findings as will assist the DSB in making the recommendations or in giving the rulings provided for in that/those agreement(s)."
>
> 2. Panels shall address the relevant provisions in any covered agreement or agreement cited by the parties to the dispute.
>
>   […].[124]

In its Report of 5 April 2019 in *Russia—Traffic in Transit*, the Panel recognized the 'inherent jurisdiction' of WTO adjudicatory bodies under the DSU.[125] It further observed that '[g]iven the absence in the DSU of any special or additional rules of procedure applying to disputes involving Article XXI GATT 1994, Russia's invocation of Article XXI(b)(iii) is within the Panel's terms of reference for the purposes of the DSU'.[126] This conclusion is reminiscent of arguments made by the ICJ in its assessment of security exceptions in FCN Agreements, where it often emphasized

---

[119] 'Decision Concerning Article XXI of the General Agreement' (2 December 1982) L/5426.

[120] The complaint was however finally rejected. GATT/CP.3/SR.22, 9, quoted from WTO, Analytical Index of the GATT (pre-1995), 606. Cf. also the presentation of GATT dispute settlement practice in Sect. 2.3.1.

[121] On GATT practice cf. Sect. 2.3.1.

[122] *Russia—Measures Concerning Traffic in Transit of Ukrainian Products*, WT/DS512, Third Party Written Submission of the European Union (8 November 2017), paras 15–16. See also the EU's emphasis on the difference between the case and the terms of reference of a previous dispute, referred to by the Russian Federation (at 4, para 17). Cf. *United States—Trade Measures affecting Nicaragua*, Report of the Panel (13 October 1986) L/6053 (not adopted), para 5.3.

[123] *Russia—Measures Concerning Traffic in Transit of Ukrainian Products*, WT/DS512, Third Party Written Submission of the European Union (8 November 2017), paras 15–16.

[124] Article 7(1) DSU.

[125] *Russia—Measures Concerning Traffic in Transit*, Report of the Panel (5 April 2019) WT/DS512/R, para 7.53.

[126] *Ibid.*, para 7.56.

the applicability of dispute settlement provisions to national security clauses.[127] It also evokes an observation made more than a decade earlier by an investment tribunal, which discussed Article XXI of the GATT in an *obiter dictum*, noting that 'the very fact that such article has not been excluded from dispute settlement is indicative of its non-self-judging nature'.[128]

2.5 The Standard of Review Under Article XXI(b) of the GATT

The Panel's finding that the security exception of the GATT does not have a self-judging character is likely to shift the focus of scholarly debate on the national security exception. The threshold issue will no longer be whether the national security clause is self-judging or not, but the determination of the standard of review which Panels—and eventually the Appellate Body—are called upon to apply in this context. The Panel Report in the case *Russia—Traffic in Transit* already provides some guidance in this fundamental regard.

Any analysis of the standard of review permissible under Article XXI(b) of the GATT must depart from the treaty text.[129] There are important differences between Article XXI and other GATT provisions allowing deviations from substantive obligations.[130] To begin with, it has been observed that—as opposed to Article XIX of the GATT—the treaty provides no specific procedural rules for the application of the national security exception.[131]

It also stands out that 'national security' was not included into the general exceptions listed in Article XX of the GATT. The separation of the two sets of exceptions is not an obvious treaty-drafting choice. The wording of the provision owes much to the debates on the draft text which the Truman Administration suggested for the ITO Charter of 1946.[132] The elements of Article XXI(b) of the GATT largely correspond to Article 37 *lit.* c, d and e of the London Draft of 1946.[133] Article 37 of the London

[127] Section 3.1 presents and discusses these decisions in more detail. It must be noted, however, that the ICJ has so far analyzed FCN treaties using a language different to the GATT.

[128] *Sempra Energy International v. Argentina*, Award (28 September 2007) ICSID Case No. ARB/02/16, para 384.

[129] *Russia—Measures Concerning Traffic in Transit of Ukrainian Products*, WT/DS512, Third Party Executive Summary of the United States of America (27 February 2018), para 7.59.

[130] For a discussion of the peculiarities of Article XXI cf. Pelc (2016), 93 *et seq* (following, however, a different approach as to the justiciability of the security exception).

[131] Cf. Desierto (2012), 161–163.

[132] Cf. Vandevelde (2017), 509.

[133] US Department of State, Preliminary Draft—Charter for the International Trade Organization of the United Nations, As Drafted at the London Meeting October 15–November 26, 1946, by the Preparatory Committee of the International Conference on Trade and Employment, 31, Art. 37 *lit.* c, d and e. For an overview of the drafting history of GATT Article XXI cf. Hahn (1996), 311–319.

Draft integrated most of the exceptions of Articles XX and XXI of the GATT in a single provision.[134]

Notably, the London Draft's exceptions did not contain a *chapeau* which sets forth general conditions for the application of the exceptions, as the final version of Article XX of the GATT does.[135] This *chapeau* is the most striking difference between Articles XX and XXI.[136] As a corollary of the *chapeau*, Article XX entails a 'two-tier test'.[137] In essence, this means that a measure must not only comply with the specific requirements for invoking one of the exceptions listed in Article XX (first tier), but also with the general requirements of the *chapeau* (second tier).[138] The *chapeau* of the general exceptions requires that the application of measures entails neither 'arbitrary or unjustifiable discrimination' nor a 'disguised restriction of international trade'.[139] This second tier has been described as 'one expression of the principle of good faith',[140] which prevents abuses of treaty rights and strikes a balance between the interests of the State invoking the exception and those of States affected by the measures.[141] The absence of an equivalent *chapeau* in Article XXI of the GATT already gives a taste of the broader discretion enjoyed by States when it comes to issues of national security.

A salient feature of Article XXI(b) of the GATT is that it provides that a WTO Member State shall not be prevented from taking actions 'which *it considers* necessary for the protection of its essential security interests'.[142] The word 'considers' has been understood to mean 'regarding something as having a specified quality' and, in

[134]US Department of State, Preliminary Draft—Charter for the International Trade Organization of the United Nations, As Drafted at the London Meeting October 15–November 26, 1946, by the Preparatory Committee of the International Conference on Trade and Employment, 31, Art. 37 *lit.* c, d and e. On the London Draft see generally Wilcox (1947), 529 *et seq.*

[135]US Department of State, Preliminary Draft—Charter for the International Trade Organization of the United Nations, As Drafted at the London Meeting October 15–November 26, 1946, by the Preparatory Committee of the International Conference on Trade and Employment, 31, Art. 37 *lit. c, d* and *e*.

[136]For an analysis of the difference between Article XX and Article XXI of the GATT cf. Pelc (2016), 93 *et seq* (discussing the *chapeau* of GATT Article XX at 129–133, but arguing at 122 that Article XXI is 'not actionable').

[137]Cf. van den Bossche (2008), 620–621; Koul AK (2018), 343.

[138]Cf. van den Bossche (2008), 620–621. The *chapeau* of Article XX reads as follows: 'Subject to the requirement that such measures are not applied in a manner which would constitute a means of arbitrary or unjustifiable discrimination between countries where the same conditions prevail, or a disguised restriction on international trade, nothing in this Agreement shall be construed to prevent the adoption or enforcement by any contracting party of measures […]'. General Agreement on Tariffs and Trade, Article XX.

[139]GATT Art. XX. For a detailed study of the *chapeau* of GATT Art. XX see Bartels (2015), 95 *et seq.*

[140]*United States—Import Prohibition of Certain Shrimp and Shrimp Products*, Report of the Appellate Body (12 October 1998) WT/DS58/AB/R, para 158.

[141]*Ibid.*, para 159.

[142]General Agreement on Tariffs and Trade, Art. XXI(b) (emphasis added).

this sense, has a noticeable subjective taint.[143] The Panel in *China—Raw Materials* underscored this subjectivity by comparing the text of Article XI:2 with the language used in Article XXI(b) of the GATT.[144] Article XI:2(a) of the GATT excludes from the scope of the general prohibition on quantitative restrictions to trade 'export prohibitions or restrictions temporarily applied to prevent or relieve critical shortages of foodstuff or other products essential to the exporting contracting party'.[145] The Panel highlighted that, in contrast to Article XXI, Article XI does not use the phrase 'which it considers necessary'.[146] It concluded that this difference indicated that a Member invoking Article XI:2(a) of the GATT cannot determine on its own whether a product is essential or not.[147] According to the Panel, '[i]f this were the case, Article XI:2 could have been drafted in a way such as Article XXI(b) of the GATT 1994'.[148]

The function of the phrase 'it considers' in the text of Article XXI requires nuanced consideration. As a preliminary matter, the phrase does not qualify all elements of the national security exception. It does not appear in *lit. c* (measures for the maintenance of international peace and security), but only in *lit. a* (disclosure of information) and *lit. b* (essential security interests). Particular attention must be drawn to *lit.* b:

> Nothing in this Agreement shall be construed
>
> [...]
>
> (b) to prevent any contracting party from taking any action *which it considers necessary* for the protection of its essential security interests
>
> (i) relating to fissionable materials or the materials from which they are derived;
>
> (ii) relating to the traffic in arms, ammunition and implements of war and to such traffic in other goods and materials as is carried on directly or indirectly for the purpose of supplying a military establishment;
>
> (iii) taken in time of war or other emergency in international relations [...].[149]

The structure of Article XXI(b) calls for a two-step assessment.[150] First, the invoking State's measure must be 'necessary for the protection of its essential security interests'. Second, it has to fit into one of the scenarios set forth in subparagraphs (i) to (iii).

The question arises as to whether the phrase 'it considers' grants a Member State discretion only with regard to whether a measure is 'necessary for the protection of its

---

[143] *Russia—Measures Concerning Traffic in Transit of Ukrainian Products*, WT/DS512, Third Party Executive Summary of the United States of America (27 February 2018) 1.

[144] *China—Measures Related to the Exportation of Various Raw Materials*, Reports of the Panel (5 July 2011) WT/DS394/R, WT/DS395/R, WT/DS398/R, para 7.276.

[145] GATT Art. XI:2(a).

[146] *China—Measures Related to the Exportation of Various Raw Materials*, Reports of the Panel (5 July 2011) WT/DS394/R, WT/DS395/R, WT/DS398/R, para 7.276.

[147] *Ibid.*

[148] *Ibid.* See also the request of the European Union to remove any reference to Art. XXI of the GATT from the Panel Report, *ibid.* para 6.22.

[149] GATT Art. XXI(b) (emphasis added).

[150] For an overview of the structure of GATT Article XXI(b) cf. Berrisch (2003), 156–158.

essential security interests', or also regarding the additional requirements established under subparagraphs (i) to (iii).[151] The Panel in *Russia—Traffic in Transit* analyzed this question in detail.[152] It concluded:

> [T]he ordinary meaning of Article XXI(b)(iii), in its context and in light of the object and purpose of the GATT 1994 and the WTO Agreement more generally, is that the adjectival clause "which it considers" in the chapeau of Article XXI(b) does not qualify the determination of the circumstances in subparagraph (iii). Rather, for action to fall within the scope of Article XXI(b), it must objectively be found to meet the requirements in one of the enumerated subparagraphs of that provision.[153]

Following this interpretation, the phrase 'it considers' refers to the noun 'action' and, as such, pertains only to the first condition for the application of Article XXI(b).[154] According to the Panel, the broad discretion a Member enjoys in determining whether a measure is 'necessary' to protect its 'essential security interests' is countered by subparagraphs (i) to (iii), which 'operate as limitative qualifying clauses'.[155] The separation of the *chapeau* of Article XXI(b) from the conditions listed in the subparagraphs implies, hence, that the assessment of each element is subject to a different standard of review.[156]

In this sense, a Panel or the Appellate Body can objectively determine whether a national security measure was 'taken in time of war or other emergency in international relations' and thus falls within the scope of Article XXI(b)(iii) of the GATT.[157] This objective assessment will include establishing the existence of the situations described in the treaty provision ('war' or 'other emergency') and the analysis of a 'chronological occurrence' ('in time of').[158] In *Russia—Traffic in Transit*, the Panel analyzed subparagraph (iii),[159] and explained:

> [A]s the existence of an emergency in international relations is an objective state of affairs, the determination of whether the action was "taken in time of" an "emergency in international relations" under subparagraph (iii) of Article XXI(b) is that of an objective fact, subject to objective determination.[160]

---

[151] For an author considering this aspect of the GATT security exception prior to the Panel Report in *Russia—Traffic in Transit* cf. Mendenhall (2012), 316.

[152] *Russia—Measures Concerning Traffic in Transit*, Report of the Panel (5 April 2019) WT/DS512/R, paras 7.62–7.82.

[153] *Ibid.*, para 7.82.

[154] Balan (2018), 15.

[155] *Russia—Measures Concerning Traffic in Transit*, Report of the Panel (5 April 2019) WT/DS512/R, para 7.65.

[156] For a brief commentary cf. Bogdanova (2019).

[157] *Russia—Measures Concerning Traffic in Transit*, Report of the Panel (5 April 2019) WT/DS512/R, para 7.70 *et seq.*

[158] *Ibid.*, paras 7.70–7.71.

[159] *Ibid.*, paras 7.66 *et seq.* For a critical analysis of this aspect of the Panel Report see Glöckle (2019), 655 *et seq.*

[160] *Russia—Measures Concerning Traffic in Transit*, Report of the Panel (5 April 2019) WT/DS512/R, para 7.77.

Analysis of the *chapeau* of GATT Article XXI(b) is characterized by the recognition of a broader margin of discretion for the invoking Member. Notwithstanding this discretion, adjudicatory bodies must still be able to examine whether a measure 'serves non-economic security interests of a State and cannot manifestly be achieved by clearly less restrictive and equally effective measures [...]'.[161] In the light of this limited standard of review, the requirements of the *chapeau* have been depicted as 'an attenuated necessity test' or 'plausibility test'.[162]

From a grammatical perspective, the phrase 'it considers' in the *chapeau* of Article XXI(b) of the GATT could also be understood as qualifying only the necessity of the measure, to the exclusion of the determination of whether there is an 'essential security interest'.[163] In *Russia—Traffic in Transit*, the Panel recognized that Members also enjoyed a reasonably broad discretion in the determination of their own essential interests of national security:

> The specific interests that are considered directly relevant to the protection of a state from such external or internal threats will depend on the particular situation and perceptions of the state in question, and can be expected to vary with changing circumstances. For these reasons, it is left, in general, to every Member to define what it considers to be its essential security interests.[164]

While acknowledging this broad margin of discretion, the Panel clarified that 'this does not mean that a Member is free to elevate every concern to that of an essential security interest'.[165] The Panel found that discretion finds its limits in good faith, as a principle that informs treaty interpretation and prevents States from abusing the security exception.[166] This view is consistent with the idea that even the broadest of exceptions must be applied in good faith, in the spirit of Article 26 of the VCLT.[167]

---

[161] Schill and Briese (2009), 120 *et seq*, in particular 137; Balan (2018), 10. In its third party submission in *Russia—Traffic in Transit*, the Australian Government formulated an slightly different standard of review: 'Rather, a panel is both empowered and required to assess whether the invoking Member *in fact* considered that action to be *necessary*; and whether that (necessary) action was *in fact* taken '*for the protection of*' a Member's essential security interests.', *Russia—Measures Concerning Traffic in Transit of Ukrainian Products*, WT/DS512, Third Party Oral Statement of Australia (25 January 2018), para 22 (emphasis in original).

[162] Balan (2018), 15–16.

[163] Cf. the discussion in *Russia—Measures Concerning Traffic in Transit*, Report of the Panel (5 April 2019) WT/DS512/R, para 7.63. Cf. also: Balan (2018), 15; Hahn (1996), 294.

[164] *Russia—Measures Concerning Traffic in Transit*, Report of the Panel (5 April 2019) WT/DS512/R, para 7.131.

[165] *Ibid.*, para 7.132.

[166] *Ibid.*, paras 7.132–7.33. On the relevance of good faith for the interpretation of treaties see generally Kolb (2017), 62 *et seq*.

[167] Cf. *Case Concerning Certain Questions of Mutual Assistance in Criminal Matters, Djibouti v France*, Judgment (4 June 2008) [2008] ICJ Rep 177, 229. In that case, the ICJ discussed the standard of review applicable under a Convention on Mutual Assistance signed between France and Djibouti in 1986, which provided that a State 'may refuse a request for mutual assistance *if it considers* that execution of the request is likely to prejudice sovereignty, [...] security, [...] ordre public or other [...] essential interests' (Art. 2, cited by the ICJ at 192, para 28). The Court (at 229, para 145) held that the State's discretion under such provision was in any case subject to the

An investment tribunal once went as far as to declare that not even a self-judging exception can exclude the examination of a measure through the prism of good faith.[168] In practice, review of security measures under the *chapeau* of GATT Article XXI must specifically focus on whether the State has misused or abused its own discretion.[169] Hence, the Panel in *Russia—Traffic in Transit* held that

> [i]t is therefore incumbent on the invoking Member to articulate the essential security interests said to arise from the emergency in international relations sufficiently enough to demonstrate their veracity. What qualifies as a sufficient level of articulation will depend on the emergency in international relations at issue. In particular, the Panel considers that the less characteristic is the "emergency in international relations" invoked by the Member, i.e. the further it is removed from armed conflict, or a situation of breakdown of law and public order (whether in the invoking Member or in its immediate surroundings), the less obvious are the defence or military interests, or maintenance of law and public order interests, that can be generally expected to arise. In such cases, a Member would need to articulate its essential security interests with greater specificity than would be required when the emergency in international relations involved, for example, armed conflict.[170]

In sum, the Panel delivered a balanced approach to the security exception. It combined the deferent standard of review applicable to the *chapeau* of Article XXI(b) and the stricter objective analysis of subparagraphs (i) to (iii). This amalgamation results in a subtle balance between a Member State's sovereign decisions about its own security, on the one hand, and the protection of the world trade system from abusive uses of the security exception, on the other.[171] Absolute deference would have the undesirable effect of exempting States from justifying or notifying trade-restrictive national security measures.[172] This would impair transparency and endanger the objectives of the world trade system.[173]

---

requirement of good faith ('[W]hile it is correct, as France claims, that the terms of Article 2 provide a State to which a request for assistance has been made with a very considerable discretion, this exercise of discretion is still subject to the obligation of good faith codified in Article 26 of the 1969 Vienna Convention on the Law of Treaties. […] This requires it to be shown that the reasons for refusal to execute the letter rogatory fell within those allowed for in Article 2. […] The Court will examine all of these elements'). For an author discussing this case in connection with Article XXI of the GATT see Balan (2018), 17.

[168] Cf. *LG&E Energy Corp.* et al. *v Argentina*, Decision on Liability (3 October 2006) ICSID Case No. ARB/02/1, para 214 (stating, in reference to Article XI of the Argentina-US BIT, that '[w]ere the Tribunal to conclude that the provision is self-judging, Argentina's determination would be subject to a good faith review anyway'). For an author analyzing the good faith requirement in detail see Eisenhut (2010), 462–4.

[169] Following the analysis of Stephan Schill and Robyn Briese, this includes the following questions: '[W]hether the factual basis of its decision was adequate and properly investigated, whether the appreciation of the governing legal framework was correct, whether the State abided by the proper procedure and whether it was guided in the exercise of discretion by relevant and pertinent considerations in view of the purpose of the treaty in question.', Schill and Briese (2009), 137.

[170] *Russia—Measures Concerning Traffic in Transit*, Report of the Panel (5 April 2019) WT/DS512/R, para 7.134 *et seq.*

[171] On this balance cf. also Sect. 2.5. Cf. also Glöckle (2019), 658.

[172] Bhala (1998), 269 *et seq.*

[173] Cf. WTO, 'Principles of the trading system', Understanding the WTO, wto.org/english/thewto_e/whatis_e/tif_e/fact2_e.htm, accessed 1 September 2019.

The Panel's approach does not only reduce the risk of abusive reliance on the security exception, but also avoids stripping States from the possibility of making a sovereign determination of their national security interests. Deference is important because, borrowing the Panel's words, the interests at stake concern 'quintessential functions of the State'.[174] As an investment arbitral tribunal put it, national security concerns the State's 'existential core'.[175] Moreover, adjudicatory bodies lack the resources and information required for a comprehensive 'reassessment' of security measures, and will typically exceed their mandate if they attempt to substitute a State's policy choice for their own.[176]

An understanding of Article XXI of the GATT as a provision that is not self-judging but calls for a limited standard of review is further consistent with the origins of the security exception.[177] Article XXI of the GATT bears striking resemblance to Article 99 of the Havana Charter of 1948,[178] which was in some degree an expression of cold war international politics.[179] The inclusion of a national security clause was one of several 'non-negotiable' conditions of the US Government for entering into the International Trade Organization (ITO).[180] It is a well-known fact that the ITO Charter never came into force due to the refusal of the US Congress to ratify the instrument.[181] Still, the negotiation record provides insights of the security exception's underlying rationale.[182]

A recent academic study of the debate within the US delegation negotiating the ITO Charter suggests that there was a deep and ever-present concern about the possible undermining effects that the security exception could have on the world trade system.[183] While some representatives of the US armed forces favored a wording that

---

[174] *Russia—Measures Concerning Traffic in Transit*, Report of the Panel (5 April 2019) WT/DS512/R, para 7.130.

[175] *CC/Devas (Mauritius) Ltd., Devas Employees Mauritius Private Ltd. and Telecom Devas Mauritius Ltd. v India*, Award on Jurisdiction and Merits (25 July 2016) PCA Case No. 2013-09, para 245. Cf. also the discussion in Sect. 3.2.3.2.

[176] Cf. the discussion in *CC/Devas (Mauritius) Ltd., Devas Employees Mauritius Private Ltd. and Telecom Devas Mauritius Ltd. v India*, Award on Jurisdiction and Merits (25 July 2016) PCA Case No. 2013-09, para 245. Cf. also Sect. 3.2.3.2.

[177] There is some controversy as regards to the intention of the treaty drafters. Thus, the United States' third-party submission in *Russia—Measures Concerning Traffic in Transit* (arguing in favor of a completely deferential standard of review) heavily relies on the historical understanding and the drafting history of the essential security clause. See *Russia—Measures Concerning Traffic in Transit of Ukrainian Products*, WT/DS512, Third Party Executive Summary of the United States of America (27 February 2018) 2 *et seq.*

[178] Cf. *Russia—Measures Concerning Traffic in Transit*, Report of the Panel (5 April 2019) WT/DS512/R, paras 7.96 *et seq.*

[179] Cf. Vandevelde (2017), 145 *et seq* (addressing the drafting history of the security exception of the ITO Charter under the suggestive heading 'the cold war comes to Geneva').

[180] Goldstein (1998), 36–37.

[181] *Ibid.*, 37.

[182] For an overview of the drafting history of GATT Art. XXI cf. Pelc (2016), 95 *et seq*; Hahn (1996), 311 *et seq.*

[183] Vandevelde (2017), 509 *et seq.*

would leave the application of the security exception exclusively in the hands of the invoking State, representatives of other departments of the US Government favored a more cautious formulation, fearing abuse by other States.[184] They agreed that each party should have discretion as to the *necessity* of the measure.[185] By contrast, such discretion would not be granted with regard to the other conditions of the security clause.[186]

In the final analysis, Article XXI of the GATT is all about balance.[187] During the 1947 Geneva negotiations, a delegate of the US Government noted that the security exception could not be as wide as to 'permit anything under the sun' and allow States to hide commercial measures behind the mask of security.[188] But neither could it be as narrow as to impair the adoption of measures which a State truly requires to safeguard its own security interests.[189]

2.6 Appraisal: In Support of a Nuanced Approach

Article XXI of the GATT has been the subject of scholarly discussion for decades. In the absence of clear guidance from WTO adjudicating bodies, the provision was often characterized as self-judging.[190] This understanding was coupled with the expectation of a politically and legally prudent behavior of Member States.[191] In 2011, a scholar observed that Article XXI had not undercut the effectiveness of the WTO Agreement, and that '[w]idespread compliance with an unreviewable, self-judging rule suggests that international law has moved beyond a primitive status'.[192]

In view of the rise of nationalist and protectionist tendencies, the growing caseload involving Article XXI of the GATT, and ongoing debates about the role of the WTO

---

[184] *Ibid.*, 510.

[185] *Ibid.*

[186] *Ibid.*

[187] Cf. Statement of the delegate of the United States, JM Leddy, UN Economic and Social Council, Second Session of the Preparatory Committee of the United Nations Conference on Trade and Employment, Verbatim Report, Thirty-Third Meeting of Commission A (24 July 1947) E/PC/T/A/PV/33, 21.

[188] *Ibid*, 20. For a discussion of this statement cf. Loewenfeld (2008), 917.

[189] Statement of the delegate of the United States, JM Leddy, UN Economic and Social Council, Second Session of the Preparatory Committee of the United Nations Conference on Trade and Employment, Verbatim Report, Thirty-Third Meeting of Commission A (24 July 1947) E/PC/T/A/PV/33, 21.

[190] For an author ascribing Article XXI of the GATT a self-judging character see Alford (2011), 702 *et seq.*

[191] Bhala (1998), 270 *et seq*. Bhala admits that there is still some risk of abuse (at 275 *et seq*).

[192] Alford (2011), 758. Cf. also Lindsay (2003), 1310–1313, particularly at 1312.

itself, it is hard to share this optimism.[193] The idea that a self judging security exception could work without compromising the effectiveness of the WTO Agreement is illusory. The illusion ends as soon as a State's security measure affects the economic interests of another State. The cautious approach of the Panel in *Russia—Traffic in Transit* is therefore most welcome. While acknowledging that there is a margin of discretion for the Member State invoking Article XXI of the GATT, it made clear that States do not enjoy unfettered discretion. As will be shown below, this approach is consistent with the prevailing view in investment arbitration.[194] A recent communication of the German Government indicates that the Panel decision is consistent with Germany's and other EU Member States' views on the GATT security exception.[195]

In line with this first Panel report, it can be concluded that most elements of Article XXI(b) of the GATT call for an objective standard of review.[196] Adjudicating bodies must assess in objective terms whether a measure actually concerns an essential security interest.[197] They must also conduct an objective analysis of whether a case fits into the situations described in subparagraphs (i) to (iii) of Article XXI(b).[198] In contrast, the State enjoys broad discretion when it comes to the choice and design of the measures it deems 'necessary' for the protection of those interests.[199] This discretion does not go as far as to exclude any form of review.[200] Even with regard to the choice and design of the measures, limited scrutiny is warranted to determine whether the State has acted in good faith.[201] WTO Panels and the Appellate Body are however expected to abstain from in-depth assessments of measures aimed at the protection of national security interests.[202].

---

[193]The mainstream view seems to have turned from optimism to pessimism. Cf. Koh (2019), 57 *et seq.* See also Voon (2019), 47–48 (specifically discussing Roger Alford's views from a present-day perspective at 47). On the discussion see also the analysis of the German Federal Parliament's Research Service, Deutscher Bundestag (2018), 4 *et seq* (also discussing Alford's views at para 7).

[194]Cf. Sects. 3.2.2 and 3.2.3.

[195]Cf. Bundesministerium für Wirtschaft und Energie, Kleine Anfrage der Abgeordneten Alexander Kulitz, Michael Theurer, Grigorios Aggelidis, weiterer Abgeordneter und der Fraktion der FDP betr.: Position der Bundesregierung zu den WTO-Reformen, BT Drucksache 19/11/11481 (6 August 2019), 8.

[196]Cf. Sect. 2.5.

[197]Cf. *ibid.*

[198]Cf. *ibid.*

[199]See *ibid.*

[200]Cf. *Russia—Measures Concerning Traffic in Transit of Ukrainian Products*, WT/DS512, Third Party Written Submission of the European Union (8 November 2017); Balan (2018), Desierto (2012), 227; Schill and Briese (2009), 106 *et seq.*

[201]Cf. Sect. 2.5.

[202]On deference cf. also Sects. 3.2.3.2 (focusing on investment law) and Chap. 5

References

Alexandroff AS, Sharma R (2005) The national security provision: GATT Article XXI. In: Appleton AE, Plummer MG (eds) The world trade organization: legal, economic and political analysis. Springer, Boston, pp 1571–1579

Alford R (2011) The self-judging WTO exception. Utah Law Rev 3:697–759

Anuradha RV (2018) Petrificus Totalus: the spell of national security! Asian J WTO & Int Health Law & Policy 13:311–332

Balan G-D (2018) On fissionable cows and the limits to the WTO security exceptions. Society of International Economic Law (SIEL), Sixth Biennial Global Conference, 2 July 2018

Bartels L (2015) The chapeau of the general exceptions in the WTO GATT and GATS agreements: a reconstruction. Am J Int Law 109:95–125

Benzing M (2010) Das Beweisrecht vor internationalen Gerichten und Schiedsgerichten in zwischenstaatlichen Streitigkeiten. Springer, Berlin, Heidelberg

Berrisch G (2003) Das Allgemeine Zoll- und Handelsabkommen (GATT 1994). In: Prieß HJ, Berrisch G (eds) WTO-Handbuch. CH Beck, München, 71–16

Bhala R (1998) National security and international trade law: what the GATT says, and what the United States does. Univ Pa J Int Law 19(2):263–317

Bogdanova I (2019) The WTO panel ruling on the national security exception: has the panel "Cut" the baby in half? EJIL Talk, 12 April 2019. https:\\ejiltalk.org/the-wto-panel-ruling-on-the-national-security-exception-has-the-panel-cut-the-baby-in-half. Accessed 1 Sept 2019

Burke-White W, von Staden A (2008) Investment protection in extraordinary times: the interpretation and application of non-precluded measures provisions in bilateral investment treaties. Va J Int Law 48(2):307–410

Charnovitz S (2018) EU can retaliate immediately against Trump's metal tariffs. International Economic Law and Policy Blog, 9 March 2018. https:\\worldtradelaw.typepad.com/ielpblog/2018/03/eu-can-retaliate-immediately-against-trumps-metal-tariffs.html. Accessed 1 Sept 2019

Communication to the Members of the GATT Council (1982) Trade Restrictions Affecting Argentina Applied for Non-Economic Reasons. L/5319//Rev. 1

Desierto DA (2012) Necessity and national emergency clauses: sovereignty in modern treaty interpretation. Brill, Nijhoff, Leiden

Deutscher Bundestag (2018) Sachstand – Auslegung des Artikel XXI GATT (Ausnahmen zur Wahrung wesentlicher nationaler Sicherheitsinteressen) durch den Dispute Settlement Body der Welthandelsorganisation. WD 2- 3000 – 073/18

Eisenhut D (2010) Sovereignty, national security and international treaty law: the standard of review of international courts and tribunals with regard to security exceptions. AVR 48:431–466

Emmes M (2019) Die Nachgeschichte des Ersten Weltkrieges: Vom Frieden, der zunächst keiner werden sollte. LIT, Berlin

Fukuyama F (1989) The end of history? Nat Interest 16:3–18

Fukuyama F (1992) The end of history and the last man. First published 1992, Free Press, New York (2006)

Fukuyama F (2018) Identity: contemporary identity politics and the struggle for recognition. Profile Books, London

Glöckle C (2019) Nationale Sicherheitsinteressen in Russia-Traffic in Transit: Die erste Panel-Entscheidung zu Art. XXI-GATT. EuZW 15:652–659

Goldsmith J, Posner E (2005) The limits of international law. Oxford University Press, Oxford

Goldstein J (1998) Creating the GATT rules: politics, institutions, and American policy. In: Howse R (ed) The world trading system: critical perspectives on the world economy, vol 1. Routledge, London, pp 22–49

Hahn M (1991) Vital Interests and the Law of GATT: an analysis of GATT's security exception. Mich J Int Law 12:558–620
Hahn M (1996) Die einseitige Aussetzung von GATT-Verpflichtungen als Repressalie. Springer, Berlin
Herdegen M (2016) Principles of international economic law, 2nd edn. Oxford University Press, Oxford
Herdegen M (2019) Völkerrecht, 18th edn. CH Beck, München
Herrmann C, Weiß W, Ohler C (2007) Welthandelsrecht. CH Beck, München
Jackson J (2006) Sovereignty, the WTO and changing fundamentals of international law. Cambridge University Press, Cambridge
Koh H (2019) The Trump administration and international law. Oxford University Press, New York
Kolb R (2017) Good faith in international law. Hart Publishing, Oxford
Koul AK (2018) Guide to the WTO and the GATT: economics, law and politics. Springer, Singapore
Krummeich G, Schröder J (eds) (2004) Der Schatten des Weltkrieges: Die Ruhrbesetzung 1923. Klartext, Essen
Lee J (2017) Commercializing national security? National security exceptions' outer parameter under GATT Article XXI. Asian J WTO Int Health Law Policy 13:277–310
Lester S (2018) How should countries retaliate against the steel/aluminum tariffs? International Economic Law and Policy Blog, 6 March 2018. https:\\worldtradelaw.typepad.com/ielpblog/2018/03/how-should-countries-retaliate-against-the-steelaluminum-tariffs.html. Accessed 1 Sept 2019
Lindsay P (2003) The ambiguity of GATT Article XXI: subtle success or rampant failure? Duke Law J 52:1277–1313
Loewenfeld A (2008) International economic law. Oxford University Press, Oxford
Matsushita M, Schoenbaum T, Mavroidis P, Hahn M (2015) The world trade organization: law, practice, and policy, 3rd edn. Oxford University Press, Oxford
Mavroidis P (2005) The general agreement on tariffs and trade. Oxford University Press, Oxford
Mavroidis P (2012) Trade in goods. Oxford University Press, Oxford
Mendenhall J (2012) The evolution of the essential security exception in U.S. trade and investment agreements. In: Sauvant K, Sachs L, Schmit Jongbloed W (eds) Sovereign investment: concerns and policy reactions. Oxford University Press, Oxford, pp 310–403
Pelc KJ (2016) Making and bending international rules. The design of exceptions and escape clauses in trade law. Cambridge University Press, New York
Sanger DE (1997) US won't offer trade testimony on Cuba Embargo. New York Times, 21 Feb 1997
Schill S, Briese R (2009) If the state considers: self-judging clauses in international dispute settlement. Max Planck Yearb UN Law Online 13:61–140
Schloemann HL, Ohlhoff S (1999) "Constitutionalization" and dispute settlement in the WTO: national security as an issue of competence. Am J Int Law 93(2):424–451
Schulze S-H (2015) Cyber-"War"-Testfall der Staatenverantwortlichkeit. Mohr Siebeck, Tübingen
Slawotsky J (2018) The national security exception in US-China FDI and trade: lessons from delaware corporate law. Chin J Comp Law 6(2):228–264
Spagnole J (1998) Can Helms-Burton be challenged under WTO? Stetson Law Rev 27:1313–1340
van den Bossche P (2008) The law and policy of the world trade organization: text. Cambridge University Press, Cambridge, Cases and Materials
Vandevelde KJ (2017) The first bilateral investment treaties: U.S. postwar friendship, commerce, and navigation treaties. Oxford University Press, New York
Voon T (2019) Can International trade recover? The security exception in WTO law: entering a new era. Am J Int Law Unbound 113:45–50
Weiler J (2018) Black Lies, White Lies and Some Uncomfortable Truths in and of the International Trading System. EJIL Talk, 25 July 2018. https:\\ejiltalk.org/black-lies-white-lies-and-some-uncomfortable-truths-in-and-of-the-international-trading-system. Accessed 1 Sept 2019

Wilcox C (1947) International trade organization: the London draft of a charter for an international trade organization. Am Econ Rev 37(2):529–541

WTO, Analytical Index of the GATT (pre-1995). https:\\wto.org/english/res_e/publications_e/ai17_e/gatt1994_e.html. Accessed 1 Sept 2019

WTO, WTO Analytical index: interpretation and application of WTO agreements. https:\\wto.org/english/res_e/publications_e/ai17_e/ai17_e.html. Accessed 1 Sept 2019

Chapter 3
The Second Generation of National Security Exceptions: Departing from the GATT Tradition?

Abstract From the 1950s onwards, national security exceptions gradually emancipated from the GATT language, particularly by eliminating the words 'it considers'. This second generation of security clauses appeared in a multitude of FCN treaties and investment agreements. These provisions entailed a reduction of States' margin of discretion and were an expression of a growing trust towards international institutions and dispute settlement mechanisms. Clauses from this generation were considered in several cases before the ICJ and investment tribunals.

3.1 Security Exceptions in FCN Agreements

Essential security provisions have been a firmly-etched element of US economic agreements since the 1950s.[1] Earlier treaties used a slightly different language, making reference to '[measures] relating to public security, or imposed for the protection of the country's essential interests in time of war or other national emergency'.[2] As such, the phrase 'essential security interests' was introduced in bilateral economic agreements in the period subsequent to the ITO Charter of 1946 and the GATT of 1947.[3] While many US Friendship, Commerce and Navigation treaties included security clauses which essentially resembled GATT Article XXI, the United States often

[1] On the origins of essential security clauses in US treaty practice see: Vandevelde (2017), 507–526.

[2] Agreement between the United States of America and Paraguay relating to Reciprocal Trade (adopted 12 September 1946, entered into force 9 April 1947) 125 UNTS 180, 196 Art. XVI(h). Similarly-worded clauses appear in other US treaties concluded in the 1940s. For an additional example see: Agreement between the United States of America and Cuba Further Supplementing and Amending the Trade Agreement Signed at Washington on 24 August 1934 as amended by the Supplementary Agreement Signed at Washington on 18 December 1939 (adopted 23 December 1941, entered into force 5 January 1942) 119 UNTS 314, 330 Art. X(g). On this treaty practice see also Vandevelde (2017), 508.

[3] Vandevelde (2017), 510–511.

S. Mantilla Blanco and A. Pehl, *National Security Exceptions in International Trade and Investment Agreements*, SpringerBriefs in Law,
https://doi.org/10.1007/978-3-030-38125-7_3

avoided the expression 'it considers' in order to 'prevent abuse of this language'.[4] For present purposes, this difference can be regarded as the most outstanding feature of the second generation of security exceptions.[5]

Security clauses in FCN treaties from the 1950s—mostly stemming from the Eisenhower Administration—have been on the spot of several international disputes. In its Judgment on the *Nicaragua* case, the International Court of Justice (ICJ) dealt with the interpretation of Article XXI(1)(d) of the US-Nicaragua FCN Treaty of 1956, which read as follows:

> [T]he present Treaty shall not preclude the application of measures:
>
> [...]
>
> (d) necessary to fulfill the obligations of a Party for the maintenance or restoration of international peace and security, or necessary to protect its essential security interests.'[6]

The initial question before the ICJ was whether the security exception posed a jurisdictional issue in the first place.[7] In a majority decision, the Court found that it had jurisdiction to rule on the security exception,[8] observing that Article XXIV(2) of the FCN Treaty granted it jurisdiction over disputes concerning the 'interpretation and application' of the Agreement.[9] According to the Court, such broad wording covered disputes pertaining to the 'interpretation and application' of Article XXI.[10]

---

[4]See *ibid.*, 511 (particularly referring to the negotiations pertaining to the US-Ireland FCN Agreement of 1948 and citing a communication of the US State Department). On the use of the phrase 'it considers' cf. also: Nolan and Sourgens (2012), 404 *et seq.*

[5]Cf. the remarks made at the Introduction. For an author emphasizing the distinction between clauses using the phrase 'it considers' and clauses avoiding such language as the basis for the applicable standard of review see Eisenhut (2010), 433–435 and 457–464.

[6]Treaty of Friendship, Commerce and Navigation between the United States of America and Nicaragua (adopted 21 January 1956, entered into force 24 May 1958) 367 UNTS 3, Art. XXI(c) and (d). Cf. also *Case Concerning Military and Paramilitary Activities in and Against Nicaragua*, Judgment on the Merits (27 June 1986) [1986] ICJ Reports 14, 115–116 para 221.

[7]The Court was divided in this regard. Cf. *Case Concerning Military and Paramilitary Activities in and Against Nicaragua*, Judgment on Jurisdiction—Dissenting Opinion of Judge Schwebel (26 November 1984) [1984] ICJ Rep 558, 635 para 128 (expressing the view that 'where a treaty excludes from its regulated reach certain areas, those areas do not fall within the jurisdictional scope of the treaty'). See also *Case Concerning Military and Paramilitary Activities in and Against Nicaragua*, Judgment on the Merits—Dissenting Opinion of Judge Schwebel (27 June 1986) [1986] ICJ Rep 259, 307 *et seq* paras 101 *et seq* (particularly at para 105). For the opposite view see *Case Concerning Military and Paramilitary Activities in and Against Nicaragua*, Judgment on Jurisdiction—Separate Opinion of Judge Nagendra Singh (26 November 1984) [1984] ICJ Rep 444, 446–448 (underscoring that the dispute settlement clause of the FCN Agreement did not exclude the security clause, and noting at p. 448 that, if the parties intended such exclusion, 'a provision to that effect would have been helpful even if it is not regarded as strictly necessary').

[8]*Case Concerning Military and Paramilitary Activities in and Against Nicaragua*, Judgment on the Merits (27 June 1986) [1986] ICJ Rep 14, 116–117 paras 222–225.

[9]Treaty of Friendship, Commerce and Navigation between the United States of America and Nicaragua (adopted 21 January 1956, entered into force 24 May 1958) 367 UNTS 3, Art. XXIV(2).

[10]*Case Concerning Military and Paramilitary Activities in and Against Nicaragua*, Judgment on the Merits (27 June 1986) [1986] ICJ Rep 14, 116 para 222.

The ICJ read the difference between the wording of the FCN treaty and the GATT as a confirmation of this understanding of the security clause.[11]

These findings logically implied rejecting the interpretation of the security exception as self-judging. The Court consistently held that 'whether a measure is necessary to protect the essential security interests of a party is not [...] purely a question for the subjective judgment of the party'.[12] The threshold issue was the extent and form of review. Noting that security clauses ultimately allow a derogation from treaty obligations, the ICJ found that they properly come into play when it is 'apparent' that a measure would otherwise constitute a treaty breach.[13] In this vein, it explained:

> [...] [The concept of essential security interests] has been subject to very broad interpretations in the past. The Court has therefore to assess whether the risk run by these "essential security interests" is reasonable, and secondly, whether the measures presented as being designed to protect these interests are not merely useful but "necessary".[14]

It has been suggested that this approach results in the application of a double standard.[15] As regards the risks, the standard is defined in terms of reasonableness and implies identifying 'patently unreasonable' assessments which could constitute a disguised 'abuse of authority'.[16] This deference recognizes that the determination of essential security risks typically belongs to the realm of politics.[17] For the evaluation of the measures adopted in response to the risk, the Court resorted to a second

---

[11] *Ibid.*

[12] *Ibid.*

[13] *Ibid.*, 117 para 225. This characterization of security clauses was later criticized by Judge Higgins in her Separate Opinion on the *Oil Platforms* case of 2003, in which she explained that—rather than allowing 'derogation' from treaty obligations—security clauses were 'in the nature of a defence or justification of acts which would otherwise constitute a breach of an obligation under the treaty concerned'. *Case Concerning Oil Platforms*, Judgment—Separate Opinion of Judge Higgins (6 November 2003) [2003] ICJ Rep 225, 226 para 4.

[14] *Case Concerning Military and Paramilitary Activities in and Against Nicaragua*, Judgment on the Merits (27 June 1986) [1986] ICJ Rep 14, 117 para 224. Applying these standards to the measures at issue, the Court rejected the US Government's security defense (at paras 281–282). Specifically, the ICJ held that President Reagan's trade embargo against Nicaragua was not justified under Article XXI because there was no proof that Nicaraguan policies turned into a threat to the essential security interests of the US in 1985 (at paras 281–282). Neither could attacks on ports and oil infrastructure be justified under the security exception (at para 282).

[15] *Case Concerning Oil Platforms*, Judgment—Separate Opinion of Judge Kooijmans (6 November 2003) [2003] ICJ Rep 246, 259–260 para 44. Cf. also *Case Concerning Oil Platforms*, Judgment—Separate Opinion of Judge Buergenthal (6 November 2003) [2003] ICJ Rep 270, 285 para 37; *Case Concerning Oil Platforms*, Judgment—Separate Opinion of Judge Owada (6 November 2003) [2003] ICJ Rep 306, 318 para 35.

[16] *Case Concerning Oil Platforms*, Judgment—Separate Opinion of Judge Kooijmans (6 November 2003) [2003] ICJ Rep 246, 259–260 para 44.

[17] *Ibid.*

standard: necessity.[18] This standard of necessity is 'stricter' than the standard of reasonableness, thus allowing a greater degree of scrutiny.[19] Interestingly, such understanding of necessity contrasts with the deferent and somewhat flexible application of necessity in the context of Article XXI of the GATT.[20]

Essential security clauses from US treaties came back to the bench decades later, in the *Oil Platforms* case. This time, the ICJ considered whether two US armed operations causing damage to Iranian oil facilities were justified under Article XX(1)(d) of the Iran-US FCN Agreement of 1955, which stated:

> The present Treaty shall not preclude the application of measures:
>
> (d) necessary to fulfil the obligations of a High Contracting Party for the maintenance or restoration of peace and security, or necessary to protect its essential security interests.[21]

The *Oil Platforms* decisions were in some respects similar, and in some respect different, from the ICJ's reasoning in *Nicaragua*. In its Judgment on Jurisdiction of 1996, the Court followed the same line of argument as in *Nicaragua* by declaring that the essential security clause provided the basis for 'a possible defence on the merits' rather than a basis for jurisdictional objections.[22] For its part, the Judgment on the Merits addressed the applicability of the essential security clause without establishing a *prima facie* breach of the treaty, as it did in the *Nicaragua* case.[23] Judge

[18] *Ibid.*

[19] *Ibid.*

[20] Cf. Sects. 2.4 and 2.5.

[21] Treaty of Amity, Economic Relations and Consular Rights between the United States of America and Iran (signed 15 August 1955, entered into force 16 June 1957) Art. XX(1)(d).

[22] *Case Concerning Oil Platforms*, Judgment on Preliminary Objection (12 December 1996) [1996] ICJ Rep 803, 811 para 20. Cf. also *Case Concerning Oil Platforms*, Judgment on Preliminary Objection—Separate Opinion of Judge Shahabuddeen (12 December 1996) [1996] ICJ Rep 822, 84; *Case Concerning Oil Platforms*, Judgment on Preliminary Objection—Separate Opinion of Judge Higgins (12 December 1996) [1996] ICJ Rep 847, 857 para 34. Cf. also *Case Concerning Oil Platforms*, Judgment (6 November 2003) [2003] ICJ Rep 161, 179 para 33; *Case Concerning Oil Platforms*, Judgment—Separate Opinion of Judge Buergenthal (6 November 2003) [2003] ICJ Rep 270, 275 para 13. Judge Schwebel strongly opposed this holding, arguing that 'Article XX is an exclusion clause [...] [s]uch an exclusion can hardly entitle the Court to assume jurisdiction over a claim that engages the essential security interests of the United States if not Iran as well'. *Case Concerning Oil Platforms*, Judgment on Preliminary Objection—Dissenting Opinion of Vice-President Schwebel (12 December 1996) [1996] ICJ Rep 874, 877. Cf. also 878 *et seq.*

[23] *Case Concerning Oil Platforms*, Judgment (6 November 2003) [2003] ICJ Rep 161, 179–181 paras 35–37. Cf. also *Case Concerning Oil Platforms*, Judgment—Declaration of Vice-President Ranjeva (6 November 2003) [2003] ICJ Rep 220, 220 paras 2–3; *Case Concerning Oil Platforms*, Judgment—Declaration of Judge Koroma (6 November 2003) [2003] ICJ Rep 223, 223–4; *Case Concerning Oil Platforms*, Judgment—Separate Opinion of Judge Parra-Aranguren (6 November 2003) [2003] ICJ Rep 241, 244 para 13. The Judgment justified this change of approach on the fact that the core of the dispute between the parties referred to the legality of the US attacks on Iran (at para 37). According to the Court, the approach followed in *Nicaragua* expressed the Court's 'freedom to select the ground on which it will base its judgment' (at para 37). At this point the Court cited the *Case Concerning the Application of the Convention of 1902 Governing the Guardianship of Infants*, Judgment (28 November 1958) [1958] ICJ Rep 55, 62. The new approach was not without controversy within the Court. Cf. *Case Concerning Oil Platforms*, Judgment—Separate Opinion of

Kooijmans seems to have captured the Court's implicit approach to this subject, when he described security clauses as 'substantive, free-standing provisions'.[24]

The *Oil Platforms* case further provided the Court with an opportunity to deal in some detail with the standard of review applicable under security clauses. According to the Court, the application of such provisions in cases pertaining to the use of force required an analysis of self-defense under general international law.[25] Thus, 'the question whether the measures taken were "necessary" overlaps with the question of their validity as acts of self-defense'.[26] This approach had a direct impact on the applicable standard of review:

Judge Higgins (6 November 2003) [2003] ICJ Rep 225, 228 *et seq*, paras 13 *et seq* (particularly at 231 *et seq* paras 25 *et seq*); *Case Concerning Oil Platforms*, Judgment—Separate Opinion of Judge Buergenthal (6 November 2003) [2003] ICJ Rep 270, 271–272 paras 5–6 and 275 *et seq* paras 13 *et seq*; *Case Concerning Oil Platforms*, Judgment—Separate Opinion of Judge Owada (6 November 2003) [2003] ICJ Rep 306, 308 para 8.

[24] *Case Concerning Oil Platforms*, Judgment—Separate Opinion of Judge Kooijmans (6 November 2003) [2003] ICJ Rep 246, 252 para 19. Cf. also 255 para 31. In the *Oil Platforms* case, the US argued that essential security clauses are neither a derogation nor a limitation of treaty obligations, but 'a substantive provision that determines, defines and delimits the obligations of the parties' (Judgment, [2003] ICJ Rep 160, 180 para 36). While the ICJ did not expressly endorse the views of the US Government, its finding suggests some sympathy for this line of argument. Kooijmans' statement confirms this observation.

[25] *Case Concerning Oil Platforms*, Judgment (6 November 2003) [2003] ICJ Rep 161, 182 para 40; cf. also the Separate Opinion of Judge Higgins, criticizing the approach of the Court: *Case Concerning Oil Platforms*, Judgment—Separate Opinion of Judge Higgins (6 November 2003) [2003] ICJ Rep 225, 236 *et seq* paras 40 *et seq*. For the debate within the ICJ cf. also *Case Concerning Oil Platforms*, Judgment—Declaration of Judge Koroma (6 November 2003) [2003] ICJ Rep 223, 223–224; *Case Concerning Oil Platforms*, Judgment—Separate Opinion of Judge Kooijmans (6 November 2003) [2003] ICJ Rep 246, 253 *et seq* paras 21 *et seq* (particularly at 257 para 35); *Case Concerning Oil Platforms*, Judgment—Separate Opinion of Judge Buergenthal (6 November 2003) [2003] ICJ Rep 270, 270 *et seq* paras 2 *et seq* (particularly at 278 *et seq* paras 20 *et seq*); *Case Concerning Oil Platforms*, Judgment—Separate Opinion of Judge Owada (6 November 2003) [2003] ICJ Rep 306, 310–311 paras 14–15 (see also 315 *et seq* paras 32 *et seq*); *Case Concerning Oil Platforms*, Judgment—Separate Opinion of Judge Simma (6 November 2003) [2003] ICJ Rep 324, 329–330 paras 9–10; *Case Concerning Oil Platforms*, Judgment—Separate Opinion of Judge Rigaux (6 November 2003) [2003] ICJ Rep 362, 374 *et seq* paras 14 *et seq*.

[26] *Case Concerning Oil Platforms*, Judgment (6 November 2003) [2003] ICJ Rep 161, 183 para 43. The Court explained that the general rules on self-defense could be resorted to as 'relevant rules of international law applicable between the parties' under Art. 31(3)(c) of the VCLT (at para 41). According to the ICJ, the *telos* of the clause could not have been to allow a party to engage in an internationally wrongful use of force against the other contracting party (at para 41). Cf. also Judge Higgins' critical analysis of the Court's use of Art. 31(3)(c) of the VCLT: *Case Concerning Oil Platforms*, Judgment—Separate Opinion of Judge Higgins (6 November 2003) [2003] ICJ Rep

> [T]he requirement of international law that measures taken avowedly in self-defence must have been necessary for that purpose is strict and objective, leaving no room for any "measure of discretion" […].[27]

In the end, the Court concluded that the US measures could not be justified as actions taken in self-defense and,[28] consequently, did not satisfy the requirements of the FCN Agreement's security exception.[29]

The FCN treaties of the Eisenhower Administration would become the subject of yet another international dispute before the ICJ, in the case *Alleged Violations of the 1955 Treaty of Amity, Economic Relations, and Consular Rights*. The United States raised an objection to the Court's jurisdiction based on Article XX of the US-Iran FCN Treaty of 1955. The Court considered this objection in its Order on Provisional Measures of 3 October 2018.[30] The Order emphasized that, as established in the *Oil Platforms* case, essential security clauses provide a defense on the merits of the dispute only, and therefore have no effect on the Court's jurisdiction.[31] The Court additionally noted that '[t]he 1955 Treaty contains no provision expressly excluding certain matters from its [the Court's] jurisdiction'.[32] It went on to state:

> Article XX, paragraph 1, defines a limited number of instances in which, notwithstanding the provisions of the Treaty, the Parties may apply certain measures. Whether and to what extent those exceptions have lawfully been relied on by the Respondent in the present case is a matter which is subject to judicial examination and, hence, forms an integral part of the material scope of the Court's jurisdiction as to the "interpretation or application" of the Treaty under Article XXI, paragraph 2.[33]

Article XX of the Iran-US FCN Treaty was also relevant for the case *Certain Iranian Assets*. In its Judgment of 13 February 2019, the Court confirmed that essential

---

225, 237 para 46 (suggesting that, by referring to the general international law on the use of force, the Court ignored the context of the FCN Agreement as a treaty of 'economic and commercial' character).

[27] *Case Concerning Oil Platforms*, Judgment (6 November 2003) [2003] ICJ Rep 161, 196 para 73. In his Separate Opinion on the case, Judge Simma expressed support for a 'particularly high demand on the standard of "necessity" embodied in Article XX' (at para 11), and explained: '[…] a measure must, first, be necessary, not just desirable or useful to protect that State's essential security interests. Second, the measure must be necessary to actually protect these interests, not just to advance or support them. Third, the measure must be necessary to protect the security interests of the State taking it. Fourth, the security interests destined to be protected must be essential. And last, of course, the measure must be concerned with the security of the Respondent itself.' *Case Concerning Oil Platforms*, Judgment—Separate Opinion of Judge Simma (6 November 2003) [2003] ICJ Rep 324, 330–331 para 11.

[28] *Case Concerning Oil Platforms*, Judgment (6 November 2003) [2003] ICJ Rep 161, 189–196 paras 57–72.

[29] *Ibid.*, 198, particularly at para 76.

[30] Cf. *Alleged Violations of the 1955 Treaty of Amity, Economic Relations, and Consular Rights*, Order/General List No. 175 (3 October 2018).

[31] *Ibid.*, 12 para 41.

[32] *Ibid.*

[33] *Ibid.*, 12 para 42.

security clauses do not establish limits on its jurisdiction, quoting previous decisions addressing the subject.[34] In his Separate Opinion on the case, Judge Ad Hoc Brower elaborated further on the interpretation of Article XX.[35] Brower observed that 'unless Article XX of the Treaty of Amity were self-judging it only could raise an issue for the merits'.[36] The Separate Opinion took into consideration that investment tribunals had regarded clauses similar to Article XX of the Iran-US FCN Treaty as non-self-judging.[37] Brower compared the wording of the FCN Treaty with Article XXI of the GATT, which he characterized as a 'paradigmatic example' of a self-judging provision, since 'it is the State Party to the GATT that is entitled to decide whether "it considers" a course of action necessary for the protection of its "essential security interests" [...]'.[38] He noted that '[s]elf-judging clauses limiting the scope of treaties on economic relations are older than the Treaty of Amity'.[39] He additionally quoted the Connally Reservation of 1946 excluding the ICJ's compulsory jurisdiction as regards 'matters which are essentially within the domestic jurisdiction of the United States of America as determined by the United States of America'.[40] Brower's conclusion was that

> [i]n 1955, the United States thus was very well aware of, and capable of drafting, self-judging clauses, which strongly suggests that, had the intention been that of making Article XX of the Treaty of Amity self-judging, the United States and Iran would have done so.[41]

Brower's analysis is appealing and is moreover consistent with the practice of investment arbitral tribunals.[42] However, the parallel between the FCN Treaty and Article XXI of the GATT is inaccurate, particularly in view of the Panel's findings in *Russia—Traffic in Transit*.[43] Still, even under the premise that the phrase 'it considers'

---

[34] *Certain Iranian Assets*, Judgment on Preliminary Objections (13 February 2019) General List No. 164, 19 para 45.

[35] *Certain Iranian Assets*, Judgment on Preliminary Objections—Separate Opinion of Judge Ad Hoc Brower (13 February 2019) General List No. 164, 4–5 paras 8–12.

[36] *Ibid.*, 4 para 9.

[37] *Ibid.*, 5 para 11, quoting *CC/Devas (Mauritius) Ltd., Devas Employees Mauritius Private Ltd. and Telecom Devas Mauritius Ltd. v India*, Award on Jurisdiction and Merits (25 July 2016) PCA Case No. 2013-09, paras 218–219. The *CC/Devas* case concerned the interpretation of Art. 11(3) of the India-Mauritius BIT.

[38] *Certain Iranian Assets*, Judgment on Preliminary Objections—Separate Opinion of Judge Ad Hoc Brower (13 February 2019) General List No. 164, 4 para 9. Brower also referred to the example of Art. XIV *bis* of the GATS (at 4 para 9).

[39] *Certain Iranian Assets*, Judgment on Preliminary Objections—Separate Opinion of Judge Ad Hoc Brower (13 February 2019) General List No. 164, 4 para 9.

[40] *Ibid.*, para 10. On the Connally Reservation cf. Stahn (2012), 662–665.

[41] *Certain Iranian Assets*, Judgment on Preliminary Objections—Separate Opinion of Judge Ad Hoc Brower (13 February 2019) General List No. 164, 4 para 10.

[42] Cf. Sect. 3.2.2.1.

[43] Cf. Sects. 2.4 and 2.5.

does not render the exception self-judging, it is certain that it points to a limited standard of review.[44]

The language of the GATT was a shaping factor for security clauses in FCN agreements negotiated in the 1950s. As Brower correctly explained, this suggests that, if negotiators had intended to exclude or significantly limit the review of security measures, they could and would have followed the GATT example. A recent historical study of US treaty practice shows that, in many cases, the decision not to include the phrase 'it considers' was a conscious decision aimed at ensuring the effectiveness of the treaty.[45] During the negotiation process of the FCN treaty with the Philippines, the United States rejected a suggestion to include a reference to 'public necessity' within the clause referring to 'national emergencies'.[46] US negotiators specifically expressed concern about the possible 'undermining effect' such language could have on the treaty.[47]

The dream of trade liberalization, coupled with the growing optimism towards economic integration that dominated trade policy during those years, might well explain the shift from clauses providing for a limited standard of review (e.g. Article XXI of the GATT) to treaty provisions allowing for a more comprehensive review of security measures.

3.2 Security Exceptions in Investment Agreements

3.2.1 A Brief Overview of Security Exceptions in Investment Agreements

Ever since the beginning of the era of bilateral investment treaties (BITs), it has been common for investment agreements to include some reference to national security.[48] Investment law scholars typically classify BIT security clauses under the broader category of provisions about non-precluded measures.[49] Just as in other frameworks,

[44]Cf. in this regard the observation of the ECJ in the *Fiocci Munizioni* case, in reference to Art. 296(1)(b) EC (now Art. 346(1)(b) TFEU): *Fiocchi Munizioni SpA v Commission of the European Communities*, Judgment of the Court of First Instance (30 September 2003) Case T-26/01, para 58 ('[...] by providing that it does not preclude a Member State from taking, in relation to the activities concerned, such measures "as it considers necessary" for the protection of its essential interests of its security, Article 296(1)(b) EC *confers on the Member States a particularly wide discretion in assessing the needs receiving such protection*'—emphasis added). On the interpretation of Art. 346 of the TFU see Kellerbauer (2019), 2052; Kahn (2017), 1080; Eisenhut (2010), 447 *et seq.*

[45]Cf. Vandevelde (2017), 508.

[46]See *ibid.*, 508–509.

[47]See *ibid.*, 509.

[48]For a general survey see: Yannaca-Small (2007), 94; see also Schreuer (2018), 13 *et seq*; Dolzer and Schreuer (2012), 189–190; Nolan and Sourgens (2012), particularly at 403.

[49]See generally: Moon (2012), 481 *et seq.*

such as the GATT or FCN treaties, these clauses operate as exceptions to investment treaty obligations by allowing the adoption of measures that would otherwise be inconsistent with the treaty.[50] This feature distinguishes them from other BIT provisions addressing extraordinary situations, such as war or national emergency clauses.[51]

The application of security clauses in the context of investment cases has so far referred to situations that significantly differ from the factual settings of the *Nicaragua* and *Oil Platforms* cases, or the *Russia—Traffic in Transit* case.[52] Against the backdrop of the Argentinean economic crisis at the edge of the 21st century, a major topic of discussion has been the possible application of security exceptions in situations of economic emergency.[53]

From another point of view, some studies suggest that national security exceptions could become particularly relevant in the context of treaties granting foreign investors the rights of entry and establishment in the same terms as nationals (pre-entry national treatment).[54] In these frameworks, security clauses facilitate enforcement of national

---

[50]On the function of essential security clauses see generally Schreuer (2018), 13. For an assessment beyond the context of IIAs see *Case Concerning Military and Paramilitary Activities in and Against Nicaragua*, Judgment on Jurisdiction and Admissibility—Separate Opinion of Judge Stephen Schwebel (26 November 1984) [1984] ICJ Rep 558, 637; *Case Concerning Military and Paramilitary Activities in and Against Nicaragua*, Judgment on the Merits—Dissenting Opinion of Judge Stephen Schwebel (27 June 1986) [1986] ICJ Rep 259, 310 para 104 (referring to Art. XXI of the US-Nicaragua FCN Treaty of 1956). For an author warning against generalizations about the intended effect of this type of clauses cf. Desierto (2012), 136–137.

[51]In *Total v Argentina*, the arbitral tribunal discussed the difference between the national emergency clause of Art. 5(3) of the Argentina-France BIT and the security clause of Art. XI of the Argentina-US BIT. See *Total S.A. v. Argentina*, Decision on Liability (27 December 2010) ICSID Case No. ARB/04/01, para 229; consider also the annulment committee's analysis of the tribunal's reasoning: *Total S.A. v. Argentina*, Decision on Annulment (1 February 2016) ICSID Case No. ARB/04/01, paras 223–228 and 284–285. Cf. also the tribunal's remarks in the *BG v Argentina* case: *BG Group Plc. v. Argentina*, Final Award (24 December 2007) UNCITRAL Arbitration, paras 381 *et seq.*

[52]Cf. Sect. 2.3. It is worth noting that a few BITs introduced language aimed at avoiding justification of certain acts of force through security clauses. See Treaty between the Government of the United States of America and the Government of the Republic of Honduras concerning the Encouragement and Reciprocal Protection of Investment (adopted 1 July 1995, entered into force 11 July 2001) Protocol, para 4 ('It is understood that nothing in paragraph 1 of Article XIV of the Treaty [...] authorizes or has the intention of authorizing either Party to that Treaty to take measures in the territory of the other Party to fulfill its obligations with respect to the maintenance or restoration of international peace or security, or the protection of its own essential security interests').

[53]For an overview see Desierto (2012), 171 *et seq.*

[54]Sornarajah (2017), 545. Cf. also the exchange of notes between Pakistan and Germany regarding the entry of German investments into Pakistan, in relation to the Germany-Pakistan BIT of 1959: 'S.A. Hasnie, Secretary at the Ministry of Finance of Pakistan, to H. von Brentano, Foreign Minister of Germany' (25 November 1959) BGBl II 1961/33, 803 ('It is our understanding that, intending to facilitate and promote investments by German nationals or companies in Pakistan, the Government of Pakistan will, prior to the entry into force of an establishment treaty the negotiation of which has been provided for, grant necessary permits to German nationals who desire to enter, stay and carry on activities in Pakistan in connection with investments by German nationals or companies

legislation by allowing investment entry restrictions on grounds of national security.[55] Such legislation is already in place in many countries, including the United States.[56] As of 2018, legislative reforms on national security and investment were also under discussion in the United Kingdom.[57]

The language of essential security clauses in BITs and investment chapters of Free Trade Agreements (FTAs), as well as their location within the treaty text, are fairly diverse.[58] Numerous treaties include a free-standing security clause.[59] In other treaties, the clause appears within a substantive treaty provision. For instance, beginning with the Germany-Pakistan BIT of 1959, it has been typical for German BITs to clarify, for the purposes of non-discrimination obligations, that 'measures taken for reasons of public security' do not constitute discriminatory treatment.[60] A similar clarification appears in the most favored nation (MFN) clause of the German Model BIT of 2008.[61] This language has been considered to be 'strongly reminiscent of exception clauses in EU law'.[62]

3.2.2 *The Review of Security Measures Under Investment Agreements and the Problem of Justiciability*

3.2.2.1 The Presumption Against National Security Exceptions' Self-judging Character

The self-judging or non-self-judging nature of security clauses has been at the heart of many investment arbitration proceedings. Despite the textual diversity of security clauses in BITs, no published decision has yet applied provisions using

except in so far as reasons of public security and order, public health or morality may warrant otherwise.'—emphasis added).

[55]Sornarajah (2017), 545 (discussing in this connection the Exon-Florio Amendment of 1988 in the United States).

[56]Cf. Foreign Investment and National Security Act (FINSA), Pub L 110-49, 121 Stat 246 (2007); Foreign Investment Risk Review Modernization Act (FIRRMA), HR 5515-538 (2018).

[57]Cf. UK Secretary of State for Business, Energy and Industrial Strategy (2018).

[58]For a detailed analysis of the wording of clauses on non-precluded measures in investment agreements see Burke-White and von Staden (2008), 326 *et seq.*

[59]See, for example: Bilateral Agreement for the Promotion and Protection of Investments between the Government of the United Kingdom of Great Britain and Northern Ireland and the Republic of Colombia (adopted 17 March 2010, entered into force 10 October 2014) Art. IV(1).

[60]Protocol to the Treaty between the Federal Republic of Germany and Pakistan for the Promotion and Protection of Investments (signed 25 November 1959, in force 28 April 1962), para 2 (specifically referring to the general non-discrimination obligation set forth in Art. 2 of the BIT).

[61]German Model BIT (2008) Art. 3(2) ('Measures that have to be taken for reasons of public security and order shall not be deemed treatment less favourable within the meaning of this article (MFN)').

[62]Dolzer and Kim (2013), 309. On this aspect of German treaties cf. also Burke-White and von Staden (2008), 326–327.

the GATT phrase 'it considers'. Available decisions concern the interpretation of second-generation security clauses. Most relevant investment cases have specifically addressed Article XI of the Argentina-US BIT of 1991, which reads as follows:

> This Treaty shall not preclude the application by either Party of measures necessary for the maintenance of public order, the fulfillment of its obligations with respect to the maintenance or restoration of international peace or security, or the Protection of its own essential security interests.[63]

This clause is one of the most litigated provisions in the history of investment treaty arbitration, as the Argentine Republic invoked it in the cases *CMS v Argentina*,[64] *Continental Casualty v Argentina*,[65] *El Paso v Argentina*,[66] *Enron v Argentina*,[67] *LG&E v Argentina*,[68] *Sempra v Argentina*,[69] and *Mobil v Argentina*.[70] The annulment committees in the cases *CMS*,[71] *Continental Casualty*,[72] *El Paso*,[73] *Enron*,[74] *Mobil*,[75] and *Sempra*[76] also addressed Article XI of the Argentina-US BIT.

Besides the Argentinean cases, national security clauses were a matter of intense discussion in the arbitral tribunal's and annulment committee's decisions in *Patrick*

[63]Treaty between the United States of America and the Argentine Republic Concerning the Reciprocal Encouragement and Protection of Investment (14 November 1991, 20 October 1994) Art. XI.

[64]*CMS Gas Transmission Company v Argentina*, Award (12 May 2005) ICSID Case No. ARB/01/8.

[65]*Continental Casualty Co. v Argentina*, Award (5 September 2008) ICSID Case No. ARB/03/9.

[66]*El Paso Energy International Co. v Argentina*, Award (31 October 2011) ICSID Case No. ARB/03/5.

[67]*Enron Corp. and Ponderosa Assets L. P. v Argentina*, Award (22 May 2007) ICSID Case No. ARB/01/3.

[68]*LG&E Energy Corp.* et al. *v Argentina*, Decision on Liability (3 October 2006) ICSID Case No. ARB/02/1.

[69]*Sempra Energy International v. Argentina*, Award (28 September 2007) ICSID Case No. ARB/02/16.

[70]*Mobil Exploration and Development Argentina Inc. Suc. Argentina and Mobil Argentina S.A. v Argentina*, Decision on Jurisdiction and Liability (10 April 2013) ICSID Case No. ARB/04/16.

[71]*CMS Gas Transmission Company v Argentina*, Decision of the Ad Hoc Committee on the Application for Annulment of the Argentine Republic (25 September 2007) ICSID Case No. ARB/01/8 (Award partially annulled).

[72]*Continental Casualty Co. v Argentina*, Decision on the Application for Partial Annulment of Continental Casualty Company and the Application for Partial Annulment of the Argentine Republic (16 September 2011) ICSID Case No. ARB/03/9 (applications for annulment dismissed).

[73]*El Paso Energy International Co. v Argentina*, Decision of the Ad Hoc Committee on the Application for Annulment of the Argentine Republic (22 September 2014) ICSID Case No. ARB/03/5 (application for annulment dismissed).

[74]*Enron Corp. and Ponderosa Assets L. P. v Argentina*, Decision on the Application for Annulment of the Argentine Republic (30 July 2010) ICSID Case No. ARB/01/3 (application for annulment dismissed).

[75]*Mobil Exploration and Development Argentina Inc. Suc. Argentina and Mobil Argentina S.A.*, Decisión sobre la solicitud de anulación de la República Argentina (8 May 2019) ICSID Case No. ARB/04/16 (application for annulment dismissed).

[76]*Sempra Energy International v Argentina*, Decision on the Argentine Republic's Application for Annulment of the Award (20 June 2010) ICSID Case No. ARB/02/16.

Mitchell v Congo.[77] The *Patrick Mitchell* case referred to the security clause of the US-Congo BIT of 1984, which is similar to Article XI of the Argentina-US BIT.[78] Another important case is *Deutsche Telekom v India*, where the arbitral tribunal conducted a thorough analysis of Article 12 of the India-Germany BIT which, albeit different, bears some resemblance to the Argentina-US BIT.[79]

Finally, one of the most important instances of application of security clauses in the past years was the award rendered in *CC/Devas v India*. The decision referred to the security clause of the Mauritius-India BIT: [80]

> The provisions of this Agreement shall not in any way limit the right of either Contracting Party to apply prohibitions or restrictions of any kind or take any other action which is directed to the protection of its essential security interests, or to the protection of public health or the prevention of diseases in pests or animals or plants.[81]

Arbitral tribunals have emphasized the importance of the exact wording used in the applicable treaty. Moreover, tribunals analyzing second-generation security clauses have indicated that the insertion of a self-judging provision into a treaty must be express. This idea is not without controversy. In *The Wimbledon*, Judges Huber and Anzilotti issued a joint dissent stating that

> [t]he right of a State to adopt the course which it considers best suited to the exigencies of its security and to the maintenance of its integrity, is so essential a right that, in case of doubt, treaty stipulations cannot be interpreted as limiting it.[82]

---

[77] *Patrick Mitchell v Congo*, Decision on the Application for Annulment of the Award (1 November 2006) ICSID Case No. ARB/99/7.

[78] Treaty between the United States of America and the Republic of Zaire concerning the Reciprocal Encouragement and Protection of Investment (signed 3 August 1984, entered into force 28 July 1989) Art. X(1) ('This Treaty shall not preclude the application by either Party of measures necessary in its territory for the maintenance of public order and morality, the fulfillment of its obligations with respect to the maintenance and restoration of international peace and security, or the, protection of its own essential security').

[79] *Deutsche Telekom AG v India*, Interim Award (13 December 2017) PCA Case No. 2014-10. The tribunal specifically noted that the treaty provision in question was 'similarly worded' as the US-Argentina BIT (at para 227). Section 3.2.3.2 discusses the wording of Art. 12 of the Germany-India BIT in more detail.

[80] *CC/Devas (Mauritius) Ltd., Devas Employees Mauritius Private Ltd. and Telecom Devas Mauritius Ltd. v India*, Award on Jurisdiction and Merits (25 July 2016) PCA Case No. 2013-09.

[81] Agreement between the Government of the Republic of Mauritius and the Government of the Republic of India for the Promotion and Protection of Investments (signed 8 September 1998, entered into force 20 June 2000) Art. 11(3).

[82] *S.S. Wimbledon*, Judgment—Dissenting Opinion by Judge Anzilotti and Judge Huber (17 August 1923) [1923] PCIJ Series A01 35, 37 para 3. This statement reflects the controversial maxim *de maximis no curat praetor*. For a critical analysis of this maxim, see Lauterpacht (1933), 158 and 176 *et seq* (emphasizing that the 'political importance' of an issue should not be relevant for determining its justiciability, and specifically discussing the views of Dionisio Anzilotti at 177). See also Lauterpacht (1927), 178 *et seq*.

In *Continental Casualty*, Argentina invoked the *Wimbledon* dissent in support of its interpretation of Article XI of the US-Argentina BIT.[83] The tribunal underscored that 'caution must be exercised in allowing a party unilaterally to escape from its treaty obligations in the absence of clear textual or contextual indications'.[84] Following the same line as the arbitrators in *Continental Casualty*, investment tribunals have consistently held that, as a rule, security clauses are only self-judging if the parties expressly ascribe such character to them.

In principle, States know how to formulate self-judging clauses and will do so whenever they see fit.[85] This holds particularly true in view of the significant difficulties which respondents have faced in their attempts to advance such interpretation of security provisions before international adjudicating bodies. In *El Paso v Argentina*, the tribunal noted that security exceptions were not necessarily self-judging.[86] The arbitrators resorted to the example of Article 15 of the European Convention on Human Rights (ECHR) ('derogation in time of emergency'), underscoring that the European Court of Human Rights (ECtHR) is empowered to scrutinize emergency derogations.[87] The *El Paso* tribunal emphasized that US negotiators could not have been unaware of the debates which security clauses precipitated in the past.[88] It further observed that 'the US has been one of the champions of self-judging clauses' and referred to the example of the Connally Reservation of 1946, included in the US declaration accepting the compulsory jurisdiction of the ICJ.[89] The arbitrators gave particular weight to the fact that the Argentina-US BIT was concluded a few years after the ICJ Judgment on the *Nicaragua* case:

> It is most unlikely that within this short time-span the US could have forgotten the lesson of *Nicaragua* which amounted to saying that if one wishes a treaty clause to be self-judging, one has to say so and to obtain the other Party's assent.[90]

Similarly, in *Mobil v Argentina* the arbitrators noted that the Argentina-US BIT was concluded shortly after the ICJ Judgment in the *Nicaragua* case, which indicated that the United States had been aware of the need for 'appropriate language' in order to

[83] *Continental Casualty Co. v Argentina*, Award (5 September 2008) ICSID Case No. ARB/03/9, para 183 n 272.

[84] *Ibid.*, para 187.

[85] Cf. also the investors' argument in *Mobil Exploration and Development Argentina Inc. Suc. Argentina and Mobil Argentina S.A. v Argentina*, Decision on Jurisdiction and Liability (10 April 2013) ICSID Case No. ARB/04/16, para 1033.

[86] *El Paso Energy International Co. v Argentina*, Award (31 October 2011) ICSID Case No. ARB/03/5, para 598.

[87] *Ibid.*

[88] *Ibid.*, para 597.

[89] *Ibid.*

[90] *Ibid.*, para 594.

introduce a self-judging security exception.[91] The tribunal found that 'at the relevant time' Article XI had not been intended to be self-judging.[92]

On another note, it is most striking that arbitral tribunals too-often draw a parallel between the first and the second generation of security exceptions, suggesting that the absence of the phrase 'it considers' speaks for the justiciability of the latter. In *Deutsche Telekom v India*, the tribunal gave weight to the fact that the BIT did not use the phrase 'considers necessary' and concluded that '[c]lear indications of the treaty would be required in order to infer that a provision is self-judging'.[93]

In the *CC/Devas v India* case of 2016, the arbitrators noted that a security clause did not allow the respondent to have the case dismissed by merely asserting that the impugned measure concerns national security.[94] According to the arbitrators, 'unless a treaty contains specific wording granting full discretion to the State to determine what it considers necessary for the protection of its security interests, national security clauses are not self-judging'.[95] They went on to note that '[s]elf-judging "essential security interests" provisions are far from being unknown in international law',[96] and mentioned the examples of GATT Article XXI and investment treaties using a similar language.[97] The common thread of the examples cited by the tribunal is the use of the phrases 'it considers' or 'it determines to be'.[98] Observing that Article 11(3) of the India-Mauritius BIT contains no such express language, the *Devas* tribunal concluded that said provision could not be regarded as self-judging.[99]

[91] *Mobil Exploration and Development Argentina Inc. Suc. Argentina and Mobil Argentina S.A. v Argentina*, Decision on Jurisdiction and Liability (10 April 2013) ICSID Case No. ARB/04/16, para 1041; cf. also para 1055.

[92] *Ibid.*, para 1041.

[93] *Deutsche Telekom AG v India*, Interim Award (13 December 2017) PCA Case No. 2014-10, para 231 (also citing the ICJ's Judgment on the Merits in the *Nicaragua* case).

[94] *CC/Devas (Mauritius) Ltd., Devas Employees Mauritius Private Ltd. and Telecom Devas Mauritius Ltd. v India*, Award on Jurisdiction and Merits (25 July 2016) PCA Case No. 2013-09, para 218.

[95] *Ibid.*, para 219.

[96] *Ibid.*, para 219 n 286.

[97] *Ibid.*

[98] *Ibid.* Among others, the tribunal referred to the example of the US-Uruguay BIT of 2005: Treaty between the United States of America and the Oriental Republic of Uruguay concerning the Encouragement and Reciprocal Protection of Investment (adopted 4 November 2005, entered into force 31 October 2006) Art. 18 ('Nothing in this Treaty shall be construed: 1. to require a Party to furnish or allow access to any information the disclosure of which it determines to be contrary to its essential security interests; or 2. to preclude a Party from applying measures that it considers necessary for the fulfilment of its obligations with respect to the maintenance or restoration of international peace or security, or the protection of its own essential security interests').

[99] *CC/Devas (Mauritius) Ltd., Devas Employees Mauritius Private Ltd. and Telecom Devas Mauritius Ltd. v India*, Award on Jurisdiction and Merits (25 July 2016) PCA Case No. 2013-09, para 219.

In November 2018, the District Court of the Hague dismissed a challenge raised by the Indian Government against the award rendered in the CC/Devas case.[100] The Dutch judgment on annulment specifically held that, in the absence of an express exclusion of the national security exception from the dispute settlement clause of the BIT, the exception had no bearing on the arbitrators' jurisdiction.[101]

The tribunals in the Argentinean cases also recognized the requirement of an express agreement on the self-judging character of security clauses, often resorting to the GATT language as a counterexample. Thus, in *CMS v Argentina*, the arbitrators observed that States' intention to include a self-judging treaty provision typically crystallized in express language and mentioned the examples of GATT Article XXI and some US BITs.[102] In *Enron v Argentina*, the arbitrators took into consideration the debate on GATT Article XXI and the ICJ's decisions in *Oil Platforms* and *Nicaragua*, and concluded that '[t]ruly exceptional and extraordinary clauses such as a self-judging provision normally must be expressly drafted to that effect'.[103]

While one may disagree with the underlying understanding of the GATT, these tribunals are right in establishing a presumption against the self-judging character of treaty provisions.[104] From a general perspective, the requirement of unequivocal language indicating the intention to introduce a self-judging clause into the treaty framework stems from a combination of two principles of treaty interpretation.

The first element is the idea that the determination of an international treaty's meaning must depart from the treaty text as such, that is, the actual words used by the parties. Article 31(1) of the VCLT enshrines a textual approach, which gives prevalence to the treaty text over the parties' 'external will'.[105] States are presumed to know what they are doing and to be capable of expressing their intentions in clear terms.[106] Moreover, as a treaty crystalizes the common will of the contracting States, its meaning cannot be reduced to unilateral determinations by one of the parties.[107] As the tribunal stated in *Mobil v Argentina*:

> The wording of the treaty is deemed to express the intention common to the Parties, and what the Parties effectively agreed to, even though a Party may have wished something

---

[100] Rechtbank Den Haag, Docket No. C-09-529140-HA ZA 17-315, ECLI:NL:RBDHA:2018:15532 (14 November 2018), paras 4.42 *et seq.*

[101] *Ibid.*

[102] *CMS Gas Transmission Company v Argentina*, Award (12 May 2005) ICSID Case No. ARB/01/8, para 370.

[103] *Enron Corp. and Ponderosa Assets L. P. v Argentina*, Award (22 May 2007) ICSID Case No. ARB/01/3, paras 335–336. A similar statement appears in the award rendered in *Sempra*. See *Sempra Energy International v Argentina*, Award (28 September 2007) ICSID Case No. ARB/02/16, para 379; cf. also the references to ICJ cases at para 383.

[104] Cf. *Sempra Energy International v Argentina*, Award (28 September 2007) ICSID Case No. ARB/02/16, para 379 ('[...] there can well be a presumption that they [treaty clauses] do not have such [self-judging] meaning in view of their exceptional nature').

[105] Dörr (2018), 579–580.

[106] Cf. *ibid.*

[107] Cf. *Sempra Energy International v Argentina*, Award (28 September 2007) ICSID Case No. ARB/02/16, para 385.

> else on one or another point. This means that, unless the contrary is specified, they are not self-judging.[108]

The second premise is the rule excluding the extensive interpretation of exceptions.[109] A good example of this line of argument appears in the *Enron v Argentina* award. The tribunal concluded that Article XI of the Argentina-US BIT was not self-judging.[110] In reaching this conclusion, it emphasized the need for a restrictive interpretation of the BIT's security clause.[111] The argument was based on a teleological interpretation of the treaty: investment agreements are precisely intended to govern 'situations of economic difficulty and hardship that require the protection of the international guaranteed rights of its beneficiaries'.[112] Similarly, in *Sempra v Argentina* the arbitrators considered the purposes of the BIT and observed that 'any interpretation resulting in an escape route from the defined obligations cannot be easily reconciled with that object and purpose'.[113] This teleological rationale also appeared in *El Paso v Argentina*, where the arbitrators noted that the BIT served the purpose of 'creating a stable and prosperous investment climate in both countries',[114] stating that '[t]hat aim could not be attained if the exceptions allowed by Article XI were considered self-judging'.[115] Besides the teleological argument, several tribunals have advanced a systematic interpretation of the BIT, underscoring that applicable dispute settlement

[108] *Mobil Exploration and Development Argentina Inc. Suc. Argentina and Mobil Argentina S.A. v Argentina*, Decision on Jurisdiction and Liability (10 April 2013) ICSID Case No. ARB/04/16, para 1037.

[109] Cf. Linderfalk (2007), 286.

[110] *Enron Corp. and Ponderosa Assets L. P. v Argentina*, Award (22 May 2007) ICSID Case No. ARB/01/3, para 339.

[111] *Ibid.*, paras 331–332.

[112] *Ibid.*, para 331. Cf. also para 332.

[113] *Sempra Energy International v Argentina*, Award (28 September 2007) ICSID Case No. ARB/02/16, para 373; cf. also para 374 ('[…] to conclude that such a determination is self-judging would definitely be inconsistent with the object and purpose […]').

[114] *El Paso Energy International Co. v Argentina*, Award (31 October 2011) ICSID Case No. ARB/03/5, para 600.

[115] *Ibid.*; see also *Mobil Exploration and Development Argentina Inc. Suc. Argentina and Mobil Argentina S.A. v Argentina*, Decision on Jurisdiction and Liability (10 April 2013) ICSID Case No. ARB/04/16, para 1049; cf. also paras 1052 and 1061–1062. See also the discussion in *Mobil Exploration and Development Argentina Inc. Suc. Argentina and Mobil Argentina S.A.*, Decisión sobre la solicitud de anulación de la República Argentina (8 May 2019) ICSID Case No. ARB/04/16, paras 89 *et seq.*

clauses do not exclude the national security exception.[116] This idea is reminiscent of ICJ decisions on FCN treaties and the Panel Report in *Russia—Traffic in Transit*.[117]

3.2.2.2 The Problem of Subsequent Practice

The analysis of essential security clauses in investment arbitration proceedings often involves a debate about the relevance of subsequent practice suggesting the self-judging character of such treaty provisions. Starting point for the debate is the influence of the security exceptions of the GATT and FCN treaties on investment treaty making.[118]

US investment treaty practice is particularly relevant in this regard.[119] The security exception of the US Model BIT of 1984 avoided the use of the GATT phrase 'it considers' and thus bore striking resemblance to security clauses from postwar FCN treaties.[120] The same pattern appeared in the security clauses of the US Model BITs of 1994 and 1998.[121] However, in the 1990s US treaty drafters began to emphasize the self-judging character of security clauses.[122] Starting point of this shift was the Protocol to the Russia-US BIT of 1992, which stated that 'whether a measure is taken by a Party to protect its essential security interests is self-judging'.[123] Treaties from

[116] *Continental Casualty Co. v Argentina*, Award (5 September 2008) ICSID Case No. ARB/03/9, para 187; *El Paso Energy International Co. v Argentina*, Award (31 October 2011) ICSID Case No. ARB/03/5, paras 592 and 609 (cf. also the tribunal's discussion of the *Nicaragua* case at para 594); *Mobil Exploration and Development Argentina Inc. Suc. Argentina and Mobil Argentina S.A. v Argentina*, Decision on Jurisdiction and Liability (10 April 2013) ICSID Case No. ARB/04/16, para 1039 (also discussing the *Nicaragua* Judgment at paras 1040–1041).

[117] *Case Concerning Military and Paramilitary Activities in and Against Nicaragua*, Judgment on the Merits (27 June 1986) [1986] ICJ Rep 14, 116 para 222. Cf. also the discussion of the *Russia—Traffic in Transit* case in section 2.4.

[118] Cf. Sect. 3.1.

[119] For an overview of the development of security exceptions in the treaty practice of the United Sates cf. Mendenhall (2012), 310 *et seq.*

[120] US Model BIT (1984) Art. X ('This Treaty shall not preclude the application by either Party of measures necessary in its jurisdiction for the maintenance of public order, the fulfillment of its obligations with respect to the maintenance or restoration of international peace or security, or the protection of its own essential security interests.').

[121] US Model BIT (1994) Art. XIV(1) ('This Treaty shall not preclude a Party from applying measures necessary for the fulfillment of its obligations with respect to the maintenance or restoration of international peace or security, or the protection of its own essential security interests.'); Art. XIV(1) of the US Model BIT of 1998 included an identical security clause.

[122] For an analysis of US treaty practice from this period see: Mendenhall (2012), 324 *et seq.*

[123] Treaty between the United States of America and the Russian Federation Concerning the Encouragement and Reciprocal Protection of Investment (adopted 17 June 1992, not in force), Protocol, Art. 8.

this period also introduced the GATT-inspired phrase 'measures that it [a Party] considers necessary for […] the protection of its own essential security interests'.[124] In the letter of submittal of the El Salvador-US BIT, the US State Department explained that '[t]his Treaty makes explicit the implicit understanding that measures to protect a Party's essential security interests are self-judging in nature'.[125] Still, the State Department added an important caveat, namely, that 'each Party would expect the provision to be applied by the other in good faith'.[126] These ideas crystalized in the US Model BITs of 2004[127] and 2012.[128]

Nonetheless, many US treaties continued to use the phrase 'measures necessary' instead of 'measures it considers necessary'.[129] Several letters of submittal state that, in the view of US drafters, those treaty clauses were self-judging in spite of the absence of the word 'considers'.[130] As will be shown below, these documents' value for the interpretation of other BIT clauses has been a hotly debated issue in investment proceedings.

In some of the arbitrations filed against Argentina, it was argued that the incorporation of the phrase 'it considers' in newer US treaties should have a bearing on the interpretation of previous agreements, such as the US-Argentina BIT of 1991.[131] In the *LG&E* case, the arbitral tribunal explained that '[t]he provisions included in the international treaty are to be interpreted in conformity with the interpretation given and agreed upon by both parties at the time of its signature'.[132] The arbitrators added

---

[124]See, for example: Treaty between the United States of America and the Republic of El Salvador concerning the Encouragement and Reciprocal Protection of Investments (adopted 10 March 1999, not in force) Art. XIV.

[125]US State Department, Letter of Submittal—El Salvador/US BIT (24 April 2000) 13.

[126]*Ibid.*; cf. in this connection also the argument of the Argentine Republic in the *Mobil* case of 2013, *Mobil Exploration and Development Argentina Inc. Suc. Argentina and Mobil Argentina S.A. v Argentina*, Decision on Jurisdiction and Liability (10 April 2013) ICSID Case No. ARB/04/16, para 1030.

[127]US Model BIT (2004) Art. 18(2) ('Nothing in this Treaty shall be construed: […] 2. to preclude a Party from applying measures that it considers necessary for the fulfillment of its obligations with respect to the maintenance or restoration of international peace or security, or the protection of its own essential security interests').

[128]US Model BIT (2012) Art. 18(2).

[129]Treaty between the Government of the United States of America and the Government of the Republic of Georgia concerning the Encouragement and Reciprocal Protection of Investments (adopted 7 March 1994, entered into force 10 August 1999) Art. XIV; Treaty between the Government of the United States of America and the Government of the Republic of Bolivia concerning the Encouragement and Reciprocal Protection of Investment (adopted 17 April 1998, entered into force 7 June 2001) Art. XIV; Treaty between the Government of the United States of America and the Government of the Republic of Honduras concerning the Encouragement and Reciprocal Protection of Investment (adopted 1 July 1995, entered into force 11 July 2001) Art. XIV.

[130]US State Department, Letter of Submittal—Georgia/ US BIT (22 June 1995) 13; US State Department, Letter of Submittal—Bolivia/US BIT (24 April 2000) 13; US State Department, Letter of Submittal—Honduras/ US BIT (1 May 2000) 13.

[131]On treaty practice regarding security exceptions see also Sect. 3.2.1.

[132]*LG&E Energy Corp.* et al. *v Argentina*, Decision on Liability (3 October 2006) ICSID Case No. ARB/02/1, para 213.

that '[i]t is not until 1992, with the ratification of the US-Russia BIT, that the United States begins to consider that the application of the essential security measures are *self-judging*'.[133] The tribunal concluded that the security clause of the Argentina-US BIT did not have a self-judging nature.[134]

In *Sempra v Argentina*, the tribunal emphasized that subsequent US treaties could not determine the meaning of clauses embedded within prior treaty frameworks.[135] Besides the temporal element, the arbitrators underscored that such treaties represented the practice of the United States and not of Argentina, noting that '[t]he view of one State does not make international law, even less so when such view is ascertained only by indirect means of interpretation or in a rather remote or general way as far as the very Treaty at issue is concerned'.[136]

In another Argentinean case, *El Paso v Argentina*, the tribunal emphasized that 'the ordinary meaning of a treaty provision is that given to its terms at the time of its conclusion'.[137] Thus, according to the tribunal, subsequent treaty negotiations were not relevant for the interpretation of the treaty.[138] The tribunal additionally analyzed whether these developments could constitute 'subsequent practice' for the purposes of Article 31(3)(b) of the VCLT.[139] In this regard, the arbitrators held that 'internal changes between the organs of one Contracting State, coupled with the silence of the other State, are not sufficient to produce an agreed practice of interpretation'.[140] They further noted that the developments in question 'did not relate to the interpretation of the 1991 BIT but to the American attitude in future negotiations with other States'.[141]

Relying on *El Paso*, the arbitrators in *Mobil v Argentina* held that subsequent treaties and model agreements were not relevant for the interpretation of Article XI of the US-Argentina BIT.[142] The tribunal stressed that the treaty's 'ordinary meaning' referred to the point in time when the instrument was adopted.[143] The arbitrators went on to explain that 'what matters is the Parties common intention *at the signature* in 1991, when negotiations had been concluded rather than subsequent events'.[144] The *Mobil* tribunal also noted that the respondent had made no attempt to establish the existence of a subsequent practice between the parties in the sense

[133] *Ibid.* (emphasis in original).

[134] *Ibid.*, para 212.

[135] *Sempra Energy International v Argentina*, Award (28 September 2007) ICSID Case No. ARB/02/16, paras 385 *et seq.*

[136] *Ibid.*, para 385.

[137] *El Paso Energy International Co. v Argentina*, Award (31 October 2011) ICSID Case No. ARB/03/5, para 591.

[138] *Ibid.*; cf. also para 609.

[139] *Ibid.*, paras 601–602.

[140] *Ibid.*, para 603.

[141] *Ibid.*, para 602.

[142] *Mobil Exploration and Development Argentina Inc. Suc. Argentina and Mobil Argentina S.A. v Argentina*, Decision on Jurisdiction and Liability (10 April 2013) ICSID Case No. ARB/04/16, para 1038.

[143] *Ibid.*

[144] *Ibid.*, para 1044.

of Article 31(3)(b) of the VCLT.[145] In addition, it held that '[d]eclarations made in connection with other BITs or the 1992 Model Treaty do not qualify as preparatory work related to the present BIT'.[146]

Tribunals have additionally expressed concern about the effect reliance on subsequent practice could have on the rights and interests of investors. In *Enron v Argentina*, the arbitrators underscored that a possible subsequent change in the contracting States' understanding of the security clause should not impair the rights of third-party beneficiaries, such as investors.[147] In *El Paso v Argentina*, the tribunal observed:

> BITs are about funds invested by foreign nationals, not about direct relationships between States. Therefore, self-judging exceptions such as that allegedly introduced into Article XI of the Argentina-US BIT by tacit consent would give extremely large power to the State on whose territory the investment was made—the reference to good faith is of little help—and expose the investors to large risks.[148]

Finally, in *Sempra v Argentina*, the tribunal also took into consideration the interests of third parties.[149] According to the tribunal, a change in the State parties' understanding of the treaty should have no effect on 'rights acquired under the treaty by investors or other beneficiaries'.[150] In the arbitrators' view, the protection of such interests finds support in the inclusion within the treaty text of sunset clauses, which protect investors' rights for a limited period of time even in the event of termination.[151]

3.2.3 The Quest for an Objective Standard of Review

Due to the consistent rejection of the self-judging character of second-generation security exceptions, the main problem posed by these treaty provisions is not justiciability, but the definition of the applicable standard of review. Tribunals generally agree on the premise that review must be objective. Still, consensus ends when

---

[145] *Ibid.*, paras 1050–1051.

[146] *Ibid.*, para 1055.

[147] *Enron Corp. and Ponderosa Assets L. P. v Argentina*, Award (22 May 2007) ICSID Case No. ARB/01/3, para 337, relying at paras 338 and 342 on *Republic of Ecuador v Occidental Exploration and Production Company* (29 April 2005) [2005] EWHC 774 (Comm), para 85. On the effects of joint interpretations by the contracting States on the rights of third-party beneficiaries see generally Pehl (2019), 206 *et seq.*

[148] *El Paso Energy International Co. v Argentina*, Award (31 October 2011) ICSID Case No. ARB/03/5, para 604.

[149] *Sempra Energy International v Argentina*, Award (28 September 2007) ICSID Case No. ARB/02/16, paras 386–387.

[150] *Ibid.*, para 386.

[151] *Ibid.* For a detailed analysis of 'sunset' or 'survival' clauses in investment treaties cf. Gatzsche (2019), 102 *et seq.*

it comes to the definition of specific parameters for scrutiny. From a conceptual standpoint, the main approaches are two: the 'state of necessity' approach and the 'autonomous standard' approach.

3.2.3.1 The 'State of Necessity' Approach

Security clauses are exceptions to treaty obligations and, as such, it is tempting to associate them with circumstances precluding wrongfulness in the general law of State responsibility. For instance, in *Patrick Mitchell v. Congo*, the annulment committee characterized Article X(1) of the Congo-US BIT as 'a provision relating to the causes for exception of liability, or, in other words, a provision which precludes the wrongfulness of the behavior of the State in certain exceptional circumstances'.[152]

In this vein, arbitral tribunals have given particular importance to the customary notion of necessity, as codified in Article 25 of the International Law Commission's Articles on State Responsibility (ILC Articles).[153] Building a bridge between the customary state of necessity and security clauses allows adjudicators to review security measures based on objective parameters. The reason is that, as expressed by the ICJ in the *Gabčíkovo-Nagymaros* case, 'the State is not the sole judge of whether those conditions [for state of necessity] have been met'.[154] In this spirit, the *Patrick Mitchell* annulment committee concluded that the security exception involved at least

[152] *Patrick Mitchell v Congo*, Decision on the Application for Annulment of the Award (1 November 2006) ICSID Case No. ARB/99/7, para 55. The committee expressly stated that the security clause '[is] not a provision which delimits the scope of application of the Treaty' (at para 55). The characterization of the security clause in the *Patrick Mitchell* case was criticized in the *Continental Casualty* award: *Continental Casualty Co. v Argentina*, Award (5 September 2008) ICSID Case No. ARB/03/9, para 167 n 242.

[153] International Law Commission, Articles on Responsibility of States for Internationally Wrongful Acts, II(2) YILC 2001, Art. 25 ('Article 25. Necessity. 1. Necessity may not be invoked by a State as a ground for precluding the wrongfulness of an act not in conformity with an international obligation of that State unless the act: (a) is the only way for the State to safeguard an essential interest against a grave and imminent peril; and (b) does not seriously impair an essential interest of the State or States towards which the obligation exists, or of the international community as a whole. 2. In any case, necessity may not be invoked by a State as a ground for precluding wrongfulness if: (a) the international obligation in question excludes the possibility of invoking necessity; or (b) the State has contributed to the situation of necessity'). Arbitral decisions relying on the customary notion of state of necessity in this context have been the subject of intense scholarly discussion. For some examples see Reinisch (2010), 148 *et seq*; Henckels (2019), 322 *et seq*; Mitchell and Henckels (2013), 103 *et seq*; Binder (2015), 447 *et seq*; Galvez (2013), 146 *et seq* (particularly at 148 *et seq*); Eisenhut (2010), 439 *et seq*; Kurz (2010), 325 *et seq*; Hoelck (2009), 440 *et seq*; Herdegen (2016a), 476–7 and 547–8; Sornarajah (2015), 308 *et seq*; Moon (2012), 481 *et seq*.

[154] *Case Concerning the Gabčíkovo-Nagymaros Project*, Judgment (25 September 1997) [1997] ICJ Rep 7, 40 para 51. This statement was later quoted in the ILC Commentary to the Articles on State Responsibility: International Law Commission, Articles on Responsibility of States for Internationally Wrongful Acts, II(2) YILC 2001, 82 (Commentary to Art. 25), para 11.

'some scrutiny by the Arbitral Tribunal'.[155] More clearly, in *EDF v Argentina* the tribunal stated that '[n]ecessity must be construed strictly and objectively, not as an easy escape hatch for host States wishing to avoid treaty obligations which prove difficult'.[156]

The perhaps clearest example of an arbitral decision linking an essential security clause to the customary notion of necessity is the award rendered in *Enron v Argentina*.[157] The arbitral tribunal held that, in the absence of an express definition of 'measures necessary for […] essential security interests' in the BIT, adjudicators were warranted to look into the customary requirements of the necessity defense.[158] In this sense, the tribunal explained, 'the Treaty thus becomes inseparable from the customary standard insofar as the conditions for the operation of state of necessity are concerned'.[159] The implication is that, as the necessity defense is not self-judging, analysis of the security exception is not merely subjective.[160] The *Enron* tribunal concluded that Argentina could not rely on state of necessity and consequently dismissed its national security defense.[161] The tribunal in *Sempra v Argentina* followed a thoroughly similar line of argument.[162]

The approach followed in the *Enron* case was, albeit creative, utterly controversial. An ICSID ad hoc committee annulled the tribunal's finding as regards to state of necessity and, noting that such finding had also been the basis of its decision on the essential security clause, also annulled the tribunal's findings about Article XI of the Argentina-US BIT.[163] Similarly, the *Sempra* annulment committee found that the arbitrators had not been justified in subjecting the BIT's security exception to the

[155] *Patrick Mitchell v Congo*, Decision on the Application for Annulment of the Award (1 November 2006) ICSID Case No. ARB/99/7, para 55 n 27, also citing in this connection *Case Concerning the Gabčíkovo-Nagymaros Project*, Judgment (25 September 1997) [1997] ICJ Rep 7, 40 para 51.

[156] *EDF International S.A., SAUR International S.A. and León Participaciones Argentinas S.A. v Argentina*, Award (12 June 2012) ICSID Case No. ARB/03/23, para 1171. It is worth noting that the *EDF* case referred to the Argentina-France BIT, which contains no essential security clause (on this difference see para 1170 of the Award). Argentina's request for annulment of the *EDF* Award focused in part on the question of necessity, but was unsuccessful, cf. *EDF International S.A., SAUR International S.A. and León Participaciones Argentinas S.A. v Argentina*, Decision—Annulment Proceeding (5 February 2016) ICSID Case No. ARB/03/23, paras 295 *et seq.*

[157] Cf. *Enron Corp. and Ponderosa Assets L. P. v Argentina*, Award (22 May 2007) ICSID Case No. ARB/01/3.

[158] *Ibid.*, para 333. According to the tribunal, an issue of *lex specialis* does not arise since 'the Treaty itself did not deal with these elements' (at para 334).

[159] *Ibid.*, para 334.

[160] *Ibid.*, para 336 (relying on the *Gabčíkovo-Nagymaros* case).

[161] *Ibid.*, para 341.

[162] *Sempra Energy International v Argentina*, Award (28 September 2007) ICSID Case No. ARB/02/16, paras 375 *et seq.* Cf. also para 388.

[163] *Enron Corp. and Ponderosa Assets L. P. v Argentina*, Decision on the Application for Annulment of the Argentine Republic (30 July 2010) ICSID Case No. ARB/01/3, paras 405–408.

customary requirements of a necessity defense.[164] For the committee, this amounted to a manifest excess of powers:

> [T]he Tribunal adopted Article 25 of the ILC Articles as the primary law to be applied, rather than Article XI of the BIT, and in so doing made a fundamental error in identifying and applying the applicable law. The Committee is therefore driven to the conclusion that the Tribunal has failed to conduct its review on the basis that the applicable legal norm is to be found in Article XI of the BIT, and that this failure constitutes an excess of powers within the meaning of the ICSID Convention.[165]

Criticism of this approach also appeared in the case *CMS v Argentina*.[166] The tribunal relied on the ICJ's finding in the *Gabčíkovo-Nagymaros* case that the State invoking necessity 'is not the sole judge' of the conditions of the necessity defense.[167] The arbitrators concluded that Article XI of the US-Argentina BIT 'is not a self-judging clause'.[168] While the annulment committee ultimately dismissed Argentina's claim concerning the tribunal's findings on the security exception, it pointed out several deficiencies in the tribunal's reasoning.[169]

The *CMS* annulment committee's analysis suggests that the mere use of the word 'necessary' in the BIT is insufficient to justify importing Article 25 of the ILC Articles into the security clause.[170] The committee identified several differences between the state of necessity codified in Article 25 of the ILC Articles and the security clause of the BIT. First, it explained, 'Article XI specifies the conditions under which the Treaty may be applied, whereas Article 25 is drafted in a negative way: it excludes the application of the State of necessity on the merits, unless certain conditions are met'.[171] Second, while necessity referred to cases where a breach has been established, the security clause excluded the application of other treaty

---

[164] Cf. *Sempra Energy International v Argentina*, Decision on the Argentine Republic's Application for Annulment of the Award (20 June 2010) ICSID Case No. ARB/02/16, paras 208–209.

[165] *Ibid.* On the 'manifest' requirement cf. paras 211 *et seq.*

[166] For an analysis of the *CMS* case's approach to necessity see Gazzini (2008), 451 *et seq.*

[167] *CMS Gas Transmission Company v Argentina*, Award (12 May 2005) ICSID Case No. ARB/01/8, para 372, citing *Case Concerning the Gabčíkovo-Nagymaros Project*, Judgment (25 September 1997) [1997] ICJ Rep 7, 40 para 51.

[168] *CMS Gas Transmission Company v Argentina*, Award (12 May 2005) ICSID Case No. ARB/01/8, para 373.

[169] *CMS Gas Transmission Company v Argentina*, Decision of the Ad Hoc Committee on the Application for Annulment of the Argentine Republic (25 September 2007) ICSID Case No. ARB/01/8, paras 127 and 136 (considering that the deficiencies in the tribunal's assessment of Art. XI of the BIT did not amount to a failure to state reasons or a manifest excess of powers under Art. 52 of the ICSID Convention).

[170] *Ibid.*, paras 129 *et seq.* Cf. also the analysis of the differences between Art. 25 of the ILC Articles and Art. XI of the US-Argentina BIT in the *Sempra* case: *Sempra Energy International v Argentina*, Decision on the Argentine Republic's Application for Annulment of the Award (20 June 2010) ICSID Case No. ARB/02/16, paras 196 *et seq.*

[171] *CMS Gas Transmission Company v Argentina*, Decision of the Ad Hoc Committee on the Application for Annulment of the Argentine Republic (25 September 2007) ICSID Case No. ARB/01/8, para 129.

provisions, so that no breach occurs in the first place.[172] Finally, the committee pointed out that the essential security clause made no reference whatsoever to the conditions set forth under the ILC Articles for state of necessity.[173]

The ad hoc committee also considered the possibility of an interplay between the security exception and the customary necessity defense. According to the committee, in case both objections are raised, the tribunal needs to follow a three-step analysis.[174] The first step is determining the existence of a *prima facie* breach of the treaty.[175] The second step is analyzing whether the operation of the security clause excludes the treaty breach.[176] The third step properly refers to the customary state of necessity, which belongs to the secondary rules of state responsibility, and could exclude responsibility for the thus established treaty breach.[177] Following this line of argument, it is clear that the application of the security clause (second step) does not involve an analysis of the conditions of state of necessity under customary international law: Even if the necessity defense is considered at the level of the primary rules of international law, the BIT's security clause prevails over Article 25 of the ILC Articles as *lex specialis*.[178]

The issue arose once again in *Continental Casualty v Argentina*, where the arbitral tribunal also underscored the differences between state of necessity and the security clause of the Argentina-US BIT.[179] The arbitrators held that measures covered by the essential security clause 'lie outside the scope of the Treaty so that the party taking it would not be in breach of the relevant BIT provision'.[180] Compared to the notion of state of necessity under Article 25 of the ILC Articles, which might refer to a broad range of international obligations, the scope of application of a security clause is quite specific.[181] In the tribunal's words:

---

[172] *Ibid.* Cf. also *El Paso Energy International Co. v. Argentina*, Award (31 October 2011) ICSID Case No. ARB/03/5, paras 553–554.

[173] *CMS Gas Transmission Company v Argentina*, Decision of the Ad Hoc Committee on the Application for Annulment of the Argentine Republic (25 September 2007) ICSID Case No. ARB/01/8, para 129.

[174] Cf. *ibid.*, para 134.

[175] *Ibid.*

[176] *Ibid.*

[177] *Ibid.*

[178] *Ibid.*, para 133.

[179] *Continental Casualty Co. v Argentina*, Award (5 September 2008) ICSID Case No. ARB/03/9, paras 162 *et seq.*

[180] *Ibid.*, para 164. Cf. also the annulment committee's analysis of this section of the award: *Continental Casualty Co. v Argentina*, Decision on the Application for Partial Annulment of Continental Casualty Company and the Application for Partial Annulment of the Argentine Republic (16 September 2011) ICSID Case No. ARB/03/9, paras 119 *et seq.*

[181] *Continental Casualty Co. v Argentina*, Award (5 September 2008) ICSID Case No. ARB/03/9, paras 166–167; cf. also the annulment committee's analysis of this section of the award: *Continental Casualty Co. v Argentina*, Decision on the Application for Partial Annulment of Continental Casualty Company and the Application for Partial Annulment of the Argentine Republic (16 September 2011) ICSID Case No. ARB/03/9, paras 116 *et seq.*

> The strict conditions to which the ILC text subjects the invocation of the defence of necessity by a State is explained by the fact that it can be invoked in any context against any international obligation. [...] This is not necessarily the case under Art. XI [...].[182]

The *Continental Casualty* tribunal noted that the analysis of state of necessity under customary law would be 'superfluous' if the security clause of the BIT were successfully invoked.[183] The tribunal analyzed the necessity of Argentina's measures based on the concept of 'necessity' developed in the context of Article XX of the GATT,[184] explaining that 'the text of Article XI derives from the parallel model clause of the U.S. FCN treaties and these treaties in turn reflect the formulation of Article XX of GATT 1947'.[185] This approach was challenged in the subsequent annulment proceedings,[186] but the annulment committee held that the issue provided no ground for annulment.[187]

In *Mobil v Argentina*, the respondent raised two separate defenses, one based on Article XI of the Argentina-US BIT, and another based on the customary necessity defense.[188] The arbitrators noted that each defense follows a different rationale.[189] Where the essential security clause is applicable, measures covered by such provision 'are excluded from the scope of the BIT'.[190] By contrast, the customary necessity defense follows a 'reverse approach': it must be first established that a breach of the BIT has taken place and, if it has, the necessity defense will come into play.[191] Recalling the *Continental* case, the arbitrators emphasized that each defense was subject to different requirements.[192]

Notwithstanding this finding, the arbitrators also recognized that 'there is a link between the two types of regulation', as both allow avoiding responsibility on grounds of national security.[193] The *Mobil* tribunal held that some elements of the customary

---

[182] *Continental Casualty Co. v Argentina*, Award (5 September 2008) ICSID Case No. ARB/03/9, para 167.

[183] *Ibid.*, para 162; cf. also *El Paso Energy International Co. v Argentina*, Award (31 October 2011) ICSID Case No. ARB/03/5, para 552; *El Paso Energy International Co. v Argentina*, Decision of the Ad Hoc Committee on the Application for Annulment of the Argentine Republic (22 September 2014) ICSID Case No. ARB/03/5, para 203.

[184] *Continental Casualty Co. v Argentina*, Award (5 September 2008) ICSID Case No. ARB/03/9, paras 192 *et seq.*

[185] *Ibid.*, para 192.

[186] *Continental Casualty Co. v Argentina*, Decision on the Application for Partial Annulment of Continental Casualty Company and the Application for Partial Annulment of the Argentine Republic (16 September 2011) ICSID Case No. ARB/03/9, paras 133 *et seq.*

[187] *Ibid.*, paras 137 *et seq.*

[188] *Mobil Exploration and Development Argentina Inc. Suc. Argentina and Mobil Argentina S.A. v Argentina*, Decision on Jurisdiction and Liability (10 April 2013) ICSID Case No. ARB/04/16, para 1014.

[189] *Ibid.*, paras 1024–1025.

[190] *Ibid.*, para 1025.

[191] *Ibid.*

[192] *Ibid.*, para 1027; cf. also para 1060.

[193] *Ibid.*, para 1028.

notion of necessity, as codified in Article 25 of the ILC Articles, could be of assistance in the application of the BIT's security exception.[194] This use of the customary necessity defense was justified on Article 31(3)(c) of the VCLT.[195] Specifically, 'the requirement under Article XI that the measures must be "necessary" presupposes that the State has at least not significantly contributed to creating the situation'.[196]

The tribunal's use of the 'non-contribution requirement' of the customary notion of state of necessity in this context was the subject of intense controversy in the subsequent annulment proceedings.[197] The *Mobil* annulment committee declared in 2019 that the tribunal's approach unjustifiably added an additional requisite to the security clause of the Argentina-US BIT, thus disregarding the carefully negotiated wording of Article XI.[198] Still, the committee considered that this error did not reach the threshold of a 'manifest' error providing a basis for annulment.[199]

In a similar spirit, the arbitral tribunal in *Deutsche Telekom v India* emphasized in 2017 the difference between the security clause of the Germany-India BIT (Article 12) and state of necessity under customary law.[200] It specifically held that the BIT's security exception 'must be interpreted in its own terms, without incorporating requirements from the customary international law state of necessity defense which are not present in the text of the Treaty'.[201] In the arbitrators' view, the conditions

---

[194] *Ibid.*, para 1060.

[195] *Ibid.*, paras 1065 *et seq.* (also discussing the *Oil Platforms* case).

[196] *Ibid.*, para 1060; cf. also paras 1062–1063 and 1070. The arbitrators further clarified that, while the respondent State bears the burden of proving fulfilment of the requirements for a successful invocation of the security exception, the investor bears the burden of proving an allegation that the State contributed to the situation (at para 1071). This question was at the heart of the dispute in the *Mobil* case (see paras 1105 *et seq*). Cf. also the Parties' arguments at paras 1072–1083 (Claimant) and 1084-1104 (Respondent). The arbitrators concluded that 'Argentina contributed to the crisis to a substantial extent, so that Article XI cannot come to its rescue' (at para 1124). Arbitrator Antonio Remiro Brotóns submitted a separate opinion which focused on this particular issue: *Mobil Exploration and Development Argentina Inc. Suc. Argentina and Mobil Argentina S.A. v Argentina*, Separate Opinion of Professor Antonio Remiro Brotóns (28 March 2013) ICSID Case No. ARB/04/16, paras 11 *et seq* (particularly at paras 65 *et seq*); cf. also *Mobil Exploration and Development Argentina Inc. Suc. Argentina and Mobil Argentina S.A. v Argentina*, Opinión Disidente del Árbitro Profesor Remiro Brotóns (26 March 2016) ICSID Case No. ARB/04/16, paras 5 *et seq*. The question of 'contribution' was also an issue in other cases against the Argentine Republic. For an overview see Tomka (2016), 490.

[197] *Mobil Exploration and Development Argentina Inc. Suc. Argentina and Mobil Argentina S.A.*, Decisión sobre la Solicitud de Anulación de la República Argentina (8 May 2019) ICSID Case No. ARB/04/16, paras 74–104.

[198] *Ibid.*, paras 96–97.

[199] *Ibid.*, para 101.

[200] *Deutsche Telekom AG v India*, Interim Award (13 December 2017) PCA Case No. 2014-10, para 228.

[201] *Ibid.*, para 229.

for a successful defense under Article 12 of the BIT were lower than the customary requirements of state of necessity.[202]

These cases show that the mere use of the term 'necessary' does not involve an incorporation by reference of the customary law on state of necessity, and does not per se exclude the self-judging character of the essential security clause. Hence, it is possible for a respondent to raise two separate and autonomous defenses, one founded on a treaty-based security exception, and another based on the customary state of necessity.

3.2.3.2 The Autonomous Standard of Review and the Problem of Deference

The rejection of the 'state of necessity' approach logically leads to the question of which standard, if not the customary notion of necessity, governs the application of second-generation security clauses in investment agreements. Arbitral tribunals have given different answers to this question. Still, they all depart from a common premise: the standard must be objective and autonomous.

The arbitral tribunal in *CC/Devas v India* delivered a detailed analysis of the deference owed to the sovereign State in the interpretation and application of a security clause. In the proceedings, India argued that the security exception of the India-Mauritius BIT limited the tribunal's scrutiny to the determination of whether a measure actually pertains to national security.[203] The respondent State further contended that an investment tribunal was not called upon to act 'as a supranational regulatory or policy-making body', further underscoring that domestic authorities were in the better position to identify a nation's security interests.[204]

For its part, the investor decried the respondent's argument as unfounded and, invoking the authority of the ICJ and other arbitral tribunals, argued that the security clause could not be considered to be 'self-judging'.[205] The arbitrators agreed that the exception lacked a self-judging nature.[206] At the same time, however, they recognized a wide margin of discretion for domestic authorities:

> An arbitral tribunal may not sit in judgment on national security matters as one any other factual dispute arising between an investor and a State. National security issues relate to the existential core of a State. An investor who wishes to challenge a State decision in that

---

[202] *Ibid.*, para 229. While recognizing that the requirements of the security defense are lower than those applicable to a necessity defense, the *Deutsche Telekom* tribunal made clear that the security exception is not self-judging (at para 231).

[203] *CC/Devas (Mauritius) Ltd., Devas Employees Mauritius Private Ltd. and Telecom Devas Mauritius Ltd. v India*, Award on Jurisdiction and Merits (25 July 2016) PCA Case No. 2013-09, para 214.

[204] *Ibid.*

[205] *Ibid.*, paras 216–217.

[206] *Ibid.*, para 219.

respect faces a heavy burden of proof, such as bad faith, absence of authority or application to measures that do not relate to essential security interests.[207]

This was a most divisive issue within the *Devas* tribunal. In a dissenting opinion, David Haigh delivered one of the most restrictive interpretations of a security exception in the history of investment claims. Haigh began by raising a legitimate concern about the possible undermining effect which a high standard of deference could have on the arbitrators' duty to make an informed decision based on a proper evaluation of the evidence submitted by the parties.[208]As regards the specifics of the security exception, Haigh set the standard at a strikingly demanding level. In the first place, he required that the 'preponderance of the evidence' indicates that measures were 'fundamentally and absolutely' aimed at the protection of national security.[209] Haigh considered that India's measures did not meet such requisite, as they had an 'undetermined' purpose and could serve a wide range of 'potential national uses'.[210] This high threshold was coupled with a second requirement: necessity. Haigh's understanding of necessity comes close to the idea of absolute necessity, in the sense of an 'unavoidable' or 'indispensable requisite'.[211] The combination of these two conditions places an excessive and unprecedented burden on the State invoking a security exception.

The standard of review applicable under Indian BITs was also a fundamental issue in the case *Deutsche Telekom v India*.[212] This decision follows a moderate approach which safeguards some degree of deference for the State, while making clear that deference does not exclude scrutiny. It may therefore be taken as a middle path between the opposite approaches taken by the arbitral tribunal and David Haigh's dissent in the *Devas* case. The claims in *Deutsche Telekom* referred to the alleged annulment of a contract between an Indian State-owned company and a subsidiary of *Deutsche Telekom*,[213] which involved the use of the S-band electromagnetic spectrum.[214] India invoked the security clause of the Germany-India BIT (Article 12), arguing that the measures in question crystalized the 'quintessential policy decision' of reserving India's S-band spectrum to 'military and other strategic use'.[215] The arbitrators focused on the wording of the security clause, which reads as follows:

[207] *Ibid.*, para 245.

[208] *CC/Devas (Mauritius) Ltd., Devas Employees Mauritius Private Ltd. and Telecom Devas Mauritius Ltd. v India*, Dissenting Opinion of David R Haigh QC (25 July 2016) PCA Case No. 2013-09, para 3.

[209] *Ibid.*, para 108.

[210] *Ibid.*, paras 98 and 110–12; cf. also para 100.

[211] *Ibid.*, para 98.

[212] *Deutsche Telekom AG v India*, Interim Award (13 December 2017) PCA Case No. 2014-10.

[213] *Ibid.*, para 5.

[214] *Ibid.*, para 6.

[215] *Ibid.*, para 183.

however held that the standard of necessity did not allow for a '*de novo*' review of the host State's measures.[225] In this sense, they recognized some 'margin of deference to the host State's determination of necessity'.[226] This deference was justified on grounds of State organs' 'proximity to the situation, expertise and competence'.[227] Still, the arbitrators also emphasized that, if the effectiveness of the treaty is to be maintained, 'the deference owed to the State cannot be unlimited'.[228] The tribunal then postulated clear criteria for the assessment of the necessity requirement:

> To assess the necessity of the measures to safeguard the state's essential security interests, the Tribunal will thus determine whether the measure was principally targeted to protect the essential security interests at stake and was objectively required in order to achieve that protection, taking into account whether the state had reasonable alternatives, less in conflict or more compliant with its international obligations.[229]

While these criteria cannot be hastily generalized and imported into different treaty frameworks, they do provide useful guidance for the future development and application of objective standards of review for security exceptions. The specific standard used in any particular case will however depend on the wording used in the respective BIT. Since treaty language is diverse, standards of review will also be diverse.

References

Binder C (2015) Circumstances Precluding Wrongfulness. In: Bungenberg M, Griebel J, Hobe S, Reinisch A (eds) International Investment Law. CH Beck, München, Hart, Oxford, Nomos, Baden-Baden, pp 442–480

Burke-White W, von Staden A (2008) Investment protection in extraordinary times: the interpretation and application of non-precluded measures provisions in bilateral investment treaties. Va J Int Law 48(2):307–410

Desierto DA (2012) Necessity and national emergency clauses: sovereignty in modern treaty interpretation. Brill Nijhoff, Leiden

Dolzer R, Schreuer C (2012) Principles of International Investment Law. Oxford University Press, Oxford

Dolzer R, Kim Y-I (2013) Germany. In: Brown C (ed) Commentaries on selected model investment treaties. Oxford University Press, Oxford, pp 289–320

Dörr O (2018) Article 31. General rule of interpretation. In: Dörr O, Schmalenbach K (eds) vienna convention on the law of treaties: a commentary, 2nd edn. Springer, Berlin, pp 557–616

Eisenhut D (2010) Sovereignty, national security and international treaty law: the standard of review of international courts and tribunals with regard to security exceptions. Arch des Völkerrechts 48:431–466

Galvez C (2013) Necessity, investor rights, and state sovereignty for NAFTA investment arbitration. Cornell Int Law J 46:143–163

---

[225] *Ibid.*

[226] *Ibid.*

[227] *Ibid.*

[228] *Ibid.*

[229] *Ibid.*, para 239.

> Nothing in this Agreement shall prevent either Contracting Party from applying prohibiti or restrictions to the extent necessary for the protection of its essential security interests for the prevention of diseases and pests in animals or plants.[216]

The Indian Government contended that States were entitled to a high degı deference when it comes to the application of measures aimed at the protecti their essential security interests.[217] While the arbitral tribunal agreed that the should enjoy some margin of discretion, it also held that the BIT did not pr for unrestricted deference, establishing clear conditions for the application (exception:

> Article 12 [...] provides for the following conditions:
>
> (i) a Contracting Party must apply a "prohibition[] or restriction[]";
>
> (ii) for the protection of a state's "essential security interests';
>
> (iii) "to the extent necessary" for such protection.[218]

The tribunal addressed the first element briefly, noting that it was not nece for the provisions or restrictions adopted by domestic authorities to be 'ge in nature'.[219] As to the second element, the arbitrators began by observing adjudicators certainly owe States some 'degree of deference' in the determinati their interests of essential security.[220] Still, they also stressed that 'deference c be unlimited'.[221] In this vein, they explained:

> [...] [T]he limits of essential security interests contemplated in Article 12 cannot be stretch beyond their natural meaning. For the Tribunal, the natural meaning of the treaty ter requires the presence of interests concerned with *security* (as opposed to other public societal interests) that are "essential", i.e. that go to the core ("the essence") of state securi In that sense, one may distinguish the "essential security interests" required for a success invocation of Article 12 from the requirement that an expropriation be carried out in the pub interest pursuant to Article 5(1) of the Treaty. Since Article 12 excludes all the obligatic of the Treaty, including the obligation to provide compensation for a lawful taking unc Article 5, it must protect something of a higher value than any "public interest" [...].[222]

In their analysis of the third requirement, the arbitrators acknowledged that the n sity of measures purportedly adopted for the protection of essential security inte is subject to arbitral scrutiny.[223] Furthermore, they found that necessity went be a mere connection between security interests and some specific measure.[224]

---

[216] Agreement between the Republic of India and the Federal Republic of Germany for the Pron and Protection of Investment (adopted 10 July 1995, entered into force 13 July 1998, termin June 2017) Art. 12.

[217] *Deutsche Telekom AG v India*, Interim Award (13 December 2017) PCA Case No. 201 paras 184–186.

[218] *Ibid.*, para 230.

[219] *Ibid.*, para 232.

[220] *Ibid.*, para 235.

[221] *Ibid.*

[222] *Ibid.*, para 236.

[223] *Ibid.*, para 238.

[224] *Ibid.*

Gatzsche K (2019) Aufhebungen und Abänderungen von Investitionsschutzabkommen. Eine Untersuchung zur Reichweite von Survival Clauses in BIT's. Nomos, Baden-Baden

Gazzini T (2008) Necessity in international investment law: some critical remarks on CMS v Argentina. JENRL 26(3):450–469

Henckels C (2019) investment treaty security exceptions, necessity and self-defense in context of armed conflict. In: Fach Gómez K, Gourgourinis A, Titi C (eds) International Investment Law and the Law of Armed Conflict. Springer, Cham, pp 319–340

Herdegen M (2016) Principles of international economic law, 2nd edn. Oxford University Press, Oxford

Hoelck M-C (2009) State of necessity and an exemption from state responsibility for investments. Max Planck UNYB 13:423–479

Kahn D-E (2017) Art. 346 AEUV. In: Geiger R, Kahn D-E, Kotzur M (eds) EUV/AEUV Kommentar. CH Beck, München, pp 1077–1079

Kellerbauer M (2019) Articles 346-348. In: Kellerbauer M, Klamert M, Tomkin J (eds) The EU treaties and the charter of fundamental rights: a commentary. Oxford University Press, Oxford, pp 2050–2057

Kurz J (2010) Adjudicating the exceptional at international investment law: security, public order and financial crisis. Int Comp Law Q 59:325–371

Lauterpacht H (1927) Private law sources and analogies of international law. Longman, Green and Co, London

Lauterpacht H (1933) The function of law in the international community. Oxford University Press, Oxford

Linderfalk U (2007) On the interpretation of treaties: the modern international law as expressed in the 1969 Vienna convention on the law of treaties. Springer, Dordrecht

Mendenhall J (2012) The evolution of the essential security exception in U.S. trade and investment agreements. In: Sauvant K, Sachs L, Schmit Jongbloed W (eds) Sovereign investment: concerns and policy reactions. Oxford University Press, Oxford, pp 310–403

Mitchell A, Henckels C (2013) Variations on a theme: comparing the concept of “Necessity” in international investment law and WTO law. Chin Int Law 14(1):93–164

Moon WJ (2012) Essential security interests in international investment agreements. J Int Econ Law 15(2):481–502

Nolan M, Sourgens F (2012) the limits of discretion? Self-judging emergency clauses in international investment agreements. In: Sauvant KP (ed) Yearbook on international law & policy 2010–2011. Oxford University Press, Oxford, pp 363–418

Pehl A (2019) Repräsentative Auslegung völkerrechtlicher Verträge. Nomos, Baden-Baden

Reinisch A (2010) Necessity in Investment Arbitration. Neth Yearb Int Law 41:137–158

Schreuer C (2018) War and peace in international investment law. Dispute Manag (TDM) 15(1)

Sornarajah M (2015) Resistance and change in the international law on foreign investment. Cambridge University Press, Cambridge

Sornarajah M (2017) The international law on foreign investment, 4th edn. Cambridge University Press, Cambridge

Stahn C (2012) Connally reservation. In: Wolfrumn R (ed) The max planck encyclopedia of public international law, vol II. Oxford University Press, Oxford, pp 662–665

Tomka P (2016) defenses based on necessity under customary international law and on necessity clauses in bilateral investment treaties. In: Kinnear M et al (eds) Building international investment law: the first 50 years of ICSID. Kluwer Law, Washington, pp 477–494

UK Secretary of State for Business (2018) Energy and industrial strategy. National Security and Investment, A Consultation on Proposed Legislative Reforms

Vandevelde KJ (2017) The first bilateral investment treaties: U.S. postwar friendship, commerce, and navigation treaties. Oxford University Press, New York

Yannaca-Small K (2007) Essential security interests under international investment law. In: OECD (ed) International investment perspectives: freedom of investment in a changing world, pp 93–134

Chapter 4
The Third Generation of National Security Exceptions: Protecting the Sovereign State

Abstract The latest treaty practice indicates a trend to introduce broadly-worded security exceptions into investment and trade agreements. This third generation is driven by the goal of ensuring that the State enjoys an ample degree of discretion in the protection of its security interests. Reluctance to interpret security exceptions as self-judging provisions has led some States to go as far as to include explicit language excluding them from the scope of dispute settlement clauses.

In the past years, the world has witnessed an increasing skepticism towards trade and investment commitments.[1] Flexible standards and broadly-drafted dispute settlement clauses are often perceived as the cause of a gradual '[e]rosion of State sovereignty'.[2] Calls for enhanced sovereignty and against international adjudication are becoming part of daily life. Prominently, the Trump Administration has expressed constant skepticism towards the extant multilateral trade system, including the WTO, initiating what could turn into a devastating trade war with other major players, such as China.[3] In addition, the United States is destabilizing the functioning of the WTO by blocking designations for current vacancies at the WTO Appellate Body.[4] The former European Commissioner for Trade, Cecilia Malmström, declared in 2018 that '[t]he multilateral system is currently under threat'.[5] A communication from the German Government of August 2019 describes the situation of the WTO as 'critical'.[6]

---

[1]For a discussion of the complex roots of the crisis of 'international liberalism' cf. Singh Grewal (2018), 596 *et seq.*

[2]Cf. Herdegen (2016), 29; cf. also 40–42.

[3]Cf. Koh (2019), 54–61. For a different perspective cf. Brewster (2019), 1422 *et seq.*

[4]For an overview cf. Suttle (2019), 399 *et seq*; Brewster (2019), 1425–1427; Brewster (2018), 3–4.

[5]Malmström (2018).

[6]Bundesministerium für Wirtschaft und Energie, Kleine Anfrage der Abgeordneten Alexander Kulitz, Michael Theurer, Grigorios Aggelidis, weiterer Abgeordneter und der Fraktion der FDP betr.: Position der Bundesregierung zu den WTO-Reformen, BT Drucksache 19/11/11481 (6 August 2019) 1.

S. Mantilla Blanco and A. Pehl, *National Security Exceptions in International Trade and Investment Agreements*, SpringerBriefs in Law,
https://doi.org/10.1007/978-3-030-38125-7_4

The overall atmosphere is one of uncertainty and skepticism. States have become increasingly cautious when entering into trade and investment treaties. In the context of trade disputes, national security has emerged as a possible vehicle for the avoidance of scrutiny over trade-restrictive measures.[7] As willingness to submit sovereign decisions to international scrutiny diminishes, security exceptions and other 'escape valves' are on the rise.[8] The goal of ensuring a wide margin of discretion for the sovereign State, and to reduce the room for adjudicatory review, dominates the current trend in the drafting of security exceptions.

In the treaty practice of some States, this trend began decades ago. Thus, while security exceptions in US postwar FCN treaties left out the phrase 'it considers', the GATT language gradually resurfaced in subsequent years.[9] The security clauses of the US Model BITs of 2004[10] and 2012[11] reflect this tendency. Similarly, the general security exception of the United States-Mexico-Canada Agreement of 2018 provides:

> Article 32.2. Essential Security.
>
> 1. Nothing in this agreement shall be construed to:
>   (a) require a Party to furnish or allow access to information the disclosure of *which it determines to be* contrary to its essential security interests; or
>   (b) preclude a Party from applying measures *that it considers* necessary for the fulfilment of its obligations with respect to the maintenance or restoration of international peace or security, or the protection of its own essential security interests.[12]

States that did not usually include security exceptions into their international treaties, such as China, have begun to use them in their most recent investment agreements.[13] The GATT continues to serve as a model for security clauses in investment treaties.[14] For instance, the Canadian Model Foreign Investment and Promotion Agreement (FIPA) includes both a list of general exceptions and a separate security exception,

---

[7]Cf. Brewster (2019), 1427 *et seq.* For a general overview of clauses introducing exceptions in economic agreements cf. de Mestral and Vanhonnaeker (2017), 79 *et seq.*

[8]On this trend see generally Henckels (2018), 2826. For the description of security clauses as 'escape valves' cf. Hahn (1991), 589.

[9]Cf. Sect. 3.2.2.2.

[10]US Model BIT (2004) Art. 18 ('Nothing in this Treaty shall be construed: 1. to require a Party to furnish or allow access to any information the disclosure of which *it determines to be contrary* to its essential security interests; or 2. to preclude a Party from applying measures that *it considers necessary* for the fulfillment of its obligations with respect to the maintenance or restoration of international peace or security, or the protection of its own security interests'—emphasis added).

[11]US Model BIT (2012) Art. 18.

[12]United States-Mexico-Canada Agreement (adopted 30 November 2019) Art. 32.1 (emphasis added).

[13]Shan and Gallagher (2013), 180 (citing the examples of ASEAN and the China-Japan-Korea Trilateral Investment Agreement).

[14]See generally Mitchell et al. (2019), 305 *et seq* (specifically referring to Canadian treaties at para 19.81).

which are respectively modelled after GATT Articles XX and XXI.[15] A few BITs introduced the phrase 'it considers', but excluded the application of the security clause in respect of specific treaty obligations, such as the non-discrimination obligation under war clauses.[16] The Colombia-Japan BIT of 2014 provides an indicative example of this approach:

> Nothing in this Agreement *other than Article 12* [Treatment in case of Strife] shall be construed: […] (b) to prevent a Contracting Party from taking any action which it considers necessary for the protection of its essential security interests […][17]

In the negotiation of EU trade and investment agreements, the European Commission has increasingly used clauses safeguarding essential security interests. Some of these security provisions bear resemblance to those found in US treaties.[18] The treaty practice of the EU is however driven by the goal of specifying the scope of security exceptions to the greatest possible extent. This has resulted in extremely detailed security exceptions. Specification has the effect of restricting both the scope of security clauses and the discretion of adjudicatory bodies.

For example, the EU-Japan Economic Partnership Agreement of 2017 contains a comprehensive clause providing general security exceptions.[19] In addition, special provisions incorporate by reference the security exceptions of Article 73 of the TRIPS Agreement.[20] The treaty also refers to national security in the specific context of technical barriers to trade.[21] As regards to investment liberalization and trade in services, another provision covers measures 'necessary to protect public security or public morals or to maintain public order'.[22] A footnote clarifies that '[t]he public security and public order exceptions may be invoked only where a genuine and sufficiently serious threat is posed to one of the fundamental interests of society'.[23] Other examples appear at many instances throughout the treaty text.[24] The EU-Japan

---

[15] Canada Model FIPA (2004) Arts. 10(1) and 10(4). On these exceptions and their similarity to the GATT see Lévesque and Newcombe (2013), 89–90.

[16] For an overview of war clauses cf. Schreuer (2013), 3 *et seq.* See also Mantilla Blanco (2019), 602 *et seq.*

[17] Agreement between Japan and the Republic of Colombia for the Liberalization, Promotion and Protection of Investment (adopted 12 September 2011, entered into force 11 September 2015) Art. 15(2) (emphasis added).

[18] See, for example: Comprehensive Economic and Trade Agreement between Canada, of the one part, and the European Union and its Member States, of the other part (adopted 30 October 2016, provisional entry into force 21 September 2017) Art. 28.6 (general national security exception).

[19] EU-Japan Economic Partnership Agreement (signed 17 July 2018, entered into force 1 January 2019), Art. 1.5.

[20] *Ibid.*, Art. 14.54.

[21] *Ibid.*, Arts. 7.5(1)(a)(i) and 7.9(2)(a).

[22] *Ibid.*, Art. 8.3(2)(a).

[23] *Ibid.*, Art. 8.3(2)(a) n 29.

[24] EU-Japan Economic Partnership Agreement (signed 17 July 2018, entered into force 1 January 2019). Thus, the section on cross-border trade in services contains a denial of benefits clause applicable where a service supplier is 'owned or controlled' by a third party national, and such third party's State of nationality is subject to measures 'related to the maintenance of international peace

EPA is not an isolated example. The Draft EU-Vietnam Investment Agreement may serve as an additional illustration of the level of detail security exceptions have reached in the Commission's drafting practice.[25]

While the aforementioned treaties evidence the proliferation of security exceptions in investment agreements as well as the use of a more specific and detailed language, they do not clarify in express terms whether such exceptions have a self-judging character. In light of the consistent rejection of an interpretation of national security clauses as self-judging in ICJ, WTO, and investment cases, it appears unlikely that any such security clauses will escape arbitral review.[26]

Nonetheless, negotiators are beginning to experiment with new forms of security exceptions. Some States have made a conscious effort to leave no room for debate, introducing security clauses that are unmistakably self-judging. These provisions have the unique feature of clarifying in unambiguous terms that security measures are not subject to international dispute settlement mechanisms. The Buenos Aires Protocol for Intra-Mercosur Investment of 2017 provides a clear example of this shift in treaty practice. The Protocol, which governs investment protection within the Southern Common Market, provides in Article 12:

> Article 12. Security Exceptions.
>
> 1. Nothing in this Protocol shall be interpreted to preclude a Member State from adopting or maintaining measures aimed at preserving public order, the fulfillment of obligations concerning the maintenance or restoration of international peace or security, the protection of its own essential security interests, or the application of its criminal laws.
> 2. The dispute settlement mechanism set forth by this Protocol *shall not be applicable* to measures a Member State adopts pursuant to paragraph 1 of this Article, or to decisions made pursuant to its national security or public order laws, which at any time prohibit or limit the making of an investment in its territory by an investor of another State Party.'[27]

---

and security, including the protection of human rights' (Art. 8.19(a)). A similar clause appears in the section concerning investment liberalization (Art. 8.13(a)).

[25] EU-Vietnam Investment Protection Agreement (negotiated text as of August 2018) Art. 4.8 ('Nothing in this Agreement shall be construed as: (a) requiring a Party to furnish information, the disclosure of which it considers contrary to its essential security interests; (b) preventing a Party from taking any action which it considers necessary for the protection of its essential security interests: (i) connected with the production of or trade in arms, munitions and war materials and relating to traffic in other goods and materials and to economic activities carried out directly or indirectly for the purpose of provisioning a military establishment; (ii) relating to the supply of services carried out directly or indirectly for the purpose of provisioning a military establishment; (iii) relating to fissionable and fusionable materials or the materials from which they are derived; or (iv) taken in time of war or other emergency in international relations').

[26] Cf. Sects. 2.4, 3.1 and 3.2.2.

[27] Authors' translation. The original Spanish text reads as follows: 'Artículo 12. Excepciones de Seguridad. 1. Nada de lo dispuesto en el presente Protocolo se interpretará en el sentido de impedir que un Estado parte adopte o mantenga medidas destinadas a preservar el orden público, el cumplimiento de sus obligaciones para el mantenimiento o la restauración de la paz o seguridad internacionales, la protección de sus propios intereses esenciales de seguridad, o aplicar las disposiciones de sus leyes penales. 2. *No estarán sujetas* al mecanismo de solución de controversias previsto en el presente Protocolo las medidas que un Estado Parte adopte en virtud del

The new Cooperation and Facilitation Agreement between Brazil and the United Arab Emirates of March 2019[28] and the Brazilian Model BIT of 2015[29] also exclude the security exception from the scope of dispute settlement provisions.

Similarly, the 2015 Indian Model BIT provides a detailed security exception, which bears resemblance to those incorporated in recent EU Investment Agreements.[30] The most striking element of the security clause appears, however, in Annex 1 to the Model BIT. This Annex explicitly declares the security exception to be 'non-justiciable':

> Where the Party asserts as a defence that conduct alleged to be a breach of its obligations under this Treaty is for the protection of its essential security interests protected by Article 33, any decision of such Party taken on such security considerations and its decision to invoke Article 33 at any time, whether before or after the commencement of arbitral proceedings shall be non-justiciable. *It shall not be open to any arbitral tribunal constituted under Chapter IV or Chapter V of this Treaty to review any such decision, even where the arbitral proceedings concern an assessment of any claim for damages and/or compensation, or an adjudication of any other issues referred to the Tribunal.*[31]

In 2016, India invited twenty-five States to jointly interpret BITs concluded between them and the Indian Government.[32] The proposed interpretative agreement restricts arbitral review in cases involving defenses under the national security exception.[33] Specifically, using a similar language as the Indian Model BIT, the statement provides that tribunals shall not

> review the merits of any such decision, even where the arbitral proceedings concern an assessment of any claim for damages and/or compensation, or an adjudication of any other issues referred to the tribunal.[34]

Based on India's Statement, the Indian Government and the Government of Bangladesh signed Joint Interpretative Notes regarding the Bangladesh-India BIT

---

párrafo 1 de este artículo, ni la decisión basada en sus leyes de seguridad nacional u orden público que en cualquier tiempo prohíba o restrinja la realización de una inversión en su territorio por un inversionista de otro Estado Parte'. Protocolo de Cooperación y Facilitación de Inversiones Intra-Mercosur (adopted 7 April 2017), https://apc.mef.gub.uy/innovaportal/file/21186/2/protocolo-de-cooperacion-y-facilitacion-de-inversiones.pdf, accessed 01 September 2019 (emphasis added).

[28] Cf. Cooperation and Facilitation Agreement between the Federative Republic of Brazil and the United Arab Emirates (adopted 15 March 2019), Art. 25(3).

[29] Cf. Brazilian Model BIT (2015), Art. 13.

[30] India Model BIT (2015), Art. 33.

[31] *Ibid.*, Annex 1 (emphasis added).

[32] Malhotra (2016).

[33] More generally on the effects of such interpretative agreements see Pehl (2019).

[34] India's Consolidated Joint Interpretative Statement (4 February 2016), para 11.1, cited in Malhotra (2016).

in 2017.[35] These include a 'Note on "essential security interests"-Article12' which 'interprets' the national security clause so as to exclude justiciability.[36]

These provisions could be a double-edged source. On the one hand, they clearly exclude arbitral review of measures justified on the security exception, hence ensuring that the State will not be subject to any form of scrutiny as regards sensitive policy choices. On the other hand, these clauses could be read as a confirmation that there is room for review in treaty frameworks where dispute settlement clauses do not expressly exclude security clauses. This might be the reason why India chose not to include the limitation of arbitral review into the national security or dispute settlement clause as such, but to attach it as an Annex to the treaty text. According to the Annex, the parties merely 'confirm' their 'understanding' that review regarding the security exception is excluded.[37] So far, this strategy has been unsuccessful. Thus, in its judgment on a challenge raised against the *Deutsche Telekom* award, the Swiss Federal Tribunal observed that—in contrast to Article 12 of the Germany-India BIT—the Indian Model BIT expressed the clear purpose of incorporating a self-judging security exception into the treaty.[38]

References

Brewster R (2018) The Trump administration and the future of the WTO. Yale J Int Law 44:1–10

Brewster R (2019) Analyzing the Trump administration's international Trade strategy. Fordham Int Law J. 42:1419–1430

de Mestral A, Vanhonnaeker L (2017) Exception clauses in mega-regionals (international investment protection and trade agreements). In: Rensmann T (ed) Mega-regional trade agreements. Springer, Cham, pp 75–119

Hahn M (1991) Vital interests and the Law of GATT: an analysis of GATT's security exception. Mich J Int Law 12:558–620

Henckels C (2018) Should investment treaties contain public policy exceptions? Boston College Law Rev 59(1):2825–2844

Herdegen M (2016) The dynamics of international law in a globalised world. Cosmopolitan values, constructive consent and diversity of legal cultures. Vittorio Klostermann, Frankfurt am Main

Koh H (2019) The Trump administration and international law. Oxford University Press, New York

Lévesque C, Newcombe A (2013) Canada. In: Brown C (ed) Commentaries on selected model investment treaties. Oxford University Press, Oxford, pp 53–130

Malhotra S (2016) India's Joint Interpretive Statement for BITs: an attempt to slay the ghosts of the Past. Investment Treaty News, 12 December 2016. https:\\iisd.org/itn/2016/12/12/indias-joint-interpretive-statement-for-bits-an-attempt-to-slay-the-ghosts-of-the-past-sarthak-malhotra. Accessed 01 September 2019

[35] Joint Interpretative Notes on the Agreement between the Government of the Republic of India and the Government of the People's Republic of Bangladesh for the Promotion and Protection of Investments (04 October 2017), https://dea.gov.in/sites/default/files/SignedCopyofJIN.pdf, accessed 01 September 2019.

[36] *Ibid.*, 6–7.

[37] India Model BIT (2015), Annex 1.

[38] Tribunal fédéral (Switzerland), *Arrêt*, 4A 65/2018 (11 December 2018), para 3.2.3.3.4.

Malmström C (2018) Speech—a multilateral investment court: a contribution to the conversation about reform of investment dispute settlement. https:\\trade.ec.europa.eu/doclib/docs/2018/november/tradoc_157512.pdf. Accessed 01 September 2019

Mantilla Blanco S (2019) Full protection and security in international investment law. Springer, Cham

Mitchell A, Munro J, Voon T (2019) Importing WTO general exceptions into international investment agreements: proportionality, myths and risks. In: Sachs L, Johnson L, Coleman J (eds) Yearbook on international investment law and policy 2017. Oxford University Press, Oxford, pp 305–355

Pehl A (2019) Repräsentative Auslegung völkerrechtlicher Verträge. Nomos, Baden-Baden

Schreuer C (2013) The protection of investments in armed conflicts. In: Baetens F (ed) Investment law within International Law. Cambridge University Press, Cambridge, pp 3–20

Shan W, Gallagher N (2013) China. In: Brown C (ed) Commentaries on selected model investment treaties. Oxford University Press, Oxford, pp 131–182

Singh Grewal D (2018) Three theses on the current crisis of international liberalism. Indiana J Global Legal Stud 25(2):595–621

Suttle O (2019) Rules and values in international adjudication. The Case of the WTO Appellate Body. ICLQ 68(2):399–441

Chapter 5
Conclusion

Abstract Recent developments have shed light on the scope of security exceptions and to some extent shifted the focus of academic debate from their alleged self-judging nature to the choice between different standards of review. At the same time, a new generation of treaties is introducing clauses which could be genuinely self-judging. No case involving such clauses has yet been adjudicated.

National security clauses are a common element of international trade and investment agreements. The recent decision of a WTO Panel in the case *Russia—Traffic in Transit* has unleashed renewed academic and practical interest in the interpretation and application of the security exception set forth in GATT Article XXI.[1] In addition to WTO law, security exceptions have gradually gained importance in other areas of international economic law, such as international investment law.

In essence, security clauses provide States with a means to protect their most fundamental security interests even where they collide with treaty obligations.[2] Referring to Article XXI of the GATT, an author observed in 2011 that the exception 'carries forward Adam Smith's great insight: defense is more important than free trade'.[3] In this sense, these provisions strike a balance between the protection of States' security interests and the overall effectiveness of treaty commitments.

This book has sought to present a holistic analysis of national security clauses in economic treaties. It went beyond the WTO Agreement and looked into the steadily growing practice of adjudicatory bodies established under other treaty frameworks. The examination of the rich adjudicatory practice of WTO dispute settlement bodies, the ICJ, and investment arbitral tribunals departed from the fundamental premise that treaty language is not univocal. The applicable standard of review can vary from one treaty to another.

Despite the need for individual consideration of the agreements and their particular language, this study identified three 'generations' of national security exceptions,

[1] Cf. Sect. 2.3.2.

[2] Cf. Sect. 2.2 *et seq.*

[3] Alford (2011), 758.

S. Mantilla Blanco and A. Pehl, *National Security Exceptions in International Trade and Investment Agreements*, SpringerBriefs in Law,
https://doi.org/10.1007/978-3-030-38125-7_5

which represent the major trends in the drafting of such treaty provisions since the end of the Second World War. The starting point was Article XXI of the GATT. In substance, the GATT exception was worded so as to grant Members some discretion regarding the adoption of trade-restrictive security measures. This is expressed by the fact that a Member may adopt measures that '*it considers* necessary for the protection of its essential security interests'.[4] Still, as the Panel Report in *Russia—Traffic in Transit* made clear, such discretion was never intended to be without limits.

The second generation coincides with a widespread optimism about liberalism. The key feature of this generation was a departure from the GATT language and, particularly, the elimination of the words 'it considers'. By avoiding this phrase, treaty drafters reduced the margin of discretion of domestic decision-makers, signaling trust towards international institutions and dispute settlement mechanisms. This type of clauses was common in postwar US FCN treaties as well as in investment treaties. There is moreover extensive case law on exceptions of this kind, as they have been constantly litigated before the ICJ and investment arbitral tribunals.

Adjudicatory practice regarding the first two generations of security clauses suggests that, contrary to a widespread view, they do not convey a self-judging character. As such, they provide no jurisdictional defense, but a defense on the merits. There is room for review. Such review is either objective or, at the very least, includes some objective elements. The precise scope of permissible scrutiny remains a hotly debated issue. The choice between a more-objective and a more-subjective standard of review promises to sow further controversy.

The third generation can be conceived as a reaction against this reluctance to accept interpretations that turn security exceptions into self-judging provisions. Some States have gone as far as to expressly include a caveat excluding the application of dispute settlement clauses in respect of security defenses. This practice prepares the ground for jurisdictional objections based on national security. It expresses a pervasive reticence towards international litigation of security measures. The proliferation of this kind of clauses goes hand in hand with the recent backlash against liberalism and international institutions.[5] Hence, there is an actual risk that national security exceptions could be misused to defend all kinds of trade-restrictive policies, undermining the effectiveness of treaty commitments.

Still, years will pass before an international dispute settlement body addresses a third-generation security exception. It is unlikely that adjudicators will ignore express language granting States a broad margin of discretion. Therefore, current trends in the drafting of security clauses could result in the application of more subjective standards of review. In some cases, adjudicators might conclude that a specific security exception has a genuine self-judging nature, providing the basis for a jurisdictional defense.

---

[4]General Agreement on Tariffs and Trade, Art. XXI(b) (emphasis added).

[5]On this backlash cf. Herdegen (2019), 11 *et seq*; Niblett (2016), 17 *et seq*.

A glance at present day world politics suggests that national security defenses will become more and more common in trade and investment dispute settlement proceedings. International adjudicating bodies should ensure that security exceptions do not deprive treaty obligations of any meaningful content. At the same time, they are expected to respect the contracting parties' intentions, allowing them to enjoy reasonable discretion in the protection of their national security interests. A balanced approach is thus not only desirable, but also necessary.

References

Alford R (2011) The self-judging WTO exception. Utah Law Rev 3:697–759

Herdegen M (2019) Der Kampf um die Weltordnung. Eine strategische Betrachtung. CH Beck, München

Niblett R (2016) Liberalism in retreat: the demise of a dream. Foreign Aff 96:17–24

The manufacturer's authorised representative in the EU is Springer Nature Customer Service Centre GmbH, Europaplatz 3, 69115 Heidelberg, Germany. If you have any concerns regarding our products, please contact ProductSafety@springernature.com

Printed and bound by CPI Group (UK) Ltd, Croydon, CR0 4YY
01/10/2026
02226351-0006